THE REAL COKE,
THE REAL STORY

THE REAL COKE,®
THE REAL STORY

THOMAS OLIVER

RANDOM HOUSE NEW YORK

Library of Congress Cataloging-in-Publication Data

Oliver, Thomas, 1950–
    The real Coke, the real story.

    Includes index.
    1. Coca-Cola Company.   2. Soft drink industry—United
States.   3. Coca-Cola Company—History.   4. Soft drink
industry—United States—History.   I. Title.
HD9349.S634C67   1986   338.7'66362'0973   86–10151
ISBN 0–394–55273–3

Manufactured in the United States of America

98765432

First Edition

To Anne Keller Dukes,
my wife,
whose editing and support have seen me
through this project and whose love
has seen me through all the rest

ACKNOWLEDGMENTS

Many thanks to Caroline Sutton, whose help in organizing and editing this book was invaluable.

Many thanks to Charlotte Mayerson for guiding me through the process of writing a book.

Thanks also to Peter Livingston, now my agent, for following Charlotte's suggestion and finding me.

I am deeply grateful for the cooperation of the Coca-Cola Company and its executives, who gave me so much of their time. A special thanks to Coca-Cola's public relations department and Carlton Curtis, and especially to Randy Donaldson, who helped me through the bureaucracy.

Thanks also to Pepsi-Cola USA and Ken Ross for his help.

Without the support and cooperation of the editors of *The Atlanta Journal* and *The Atlanta Constitution*, this book would have been impossible.

And finally many thanks to my family and friends, whose moral support was needed and freely given.

THOMAS OLIVER

CONTENTS

CONTENTS

THE REAL COKE,
THE REAL STORY

PROLOGUE

On April 23, 1985, the top executives of the Coca-Cola Company held a press conference in New York City. News had leaked out that Coke, the king of soft drinks, would no longer be produced. In its place the Coca-Cola Company would offer a new drink with a new taste and would dare to call it by the old name, Coca-Cola. At the Vivian Beaumont Theater in Lincoln Center, some two hundred reporters, photographers, and cameramen eagerly awaited confirmation of the sensational news, while hundreds more participated via satellite hookup in Los Angeles, Chicago, Houston, Atlanta, and Toronto.

Why, after all, was there so much interest? Because Coke is more than just a soft drink. What the famous Kansas newspaper editor William Allen White wrote is true: "Coca-Cola is the sublimated essence of all that America stands for. A decent thing, honestly made, [and] universally distributed."

Coke had grown up with twentieth-century America, where

rites of passage are marked by moving from sipping Coke as a soda pop to mixing it with rum as an adult's elixir. And that famous Coca-Cola logo appears on signs and billboards in virtually every other country as well, linking America to the rest of the world and looming as large as a symbol of the United States as the Statue of Liberty. Coke is so strongly identified with the United States that when countries fall out with us politically, Coke's exile sometimes closely follows the expulsion of our ambassador. Antiwestern insurgents often identify Coca-Cola as the most visible example of capitalism in their countries and have blown up or taken over more than one Coca-Cola bottling plant in retaliation for some alleged grievance.

At home, Coke is more than a drink: it is sandlot baseball, high school pep rallies, that first driver's license, hot rods, swimming pools, and street dances. It is the pause that refreshes and reminds us all of the good times, and it has even helped us through some of the bad.

With that passionate public concern in the background, amid the television lights and the red wash of Coca-Cola banners, on that April day in 1985, Roberto C. Goizueta, the chairman and chief executive officer of Coca-Cola, announced that the "best has been made even better." The world's largest soft-drink company had developed an improved taste for the world's number-one soft drink. After one hundred years, Coke would have a new taste.

Goizueta said that his company's decision to make the change was based on nearly two hundred thousand consumer taste tests, which had revealed a resounding preference for the new flavor. "To market research experts, to our bottlers, and to the retail trade, these numbers represent a staggering superiority," declared Donald R. Keough, the president of Coca-Cola. In no uncertain terms Goizueta told the press that the bold change was backed by tremendous confidence and enthusiasm on the part of the Coca-Cola Company. It was "the surest move the company ever made," he said.

And so the new Coke was launched—and the reaction of the American people was immediate and violent: three months of unrelenting protest against the loss of Coke. So fierce was the reaction across the country that it forced a response from the Coca-Cola Company. On July 11, 1985, Goizueta and Keough called another press conference. This one took place at the company's headquarters in Atlanta, and this time there was no hoopla, no dog-and-pony show, no bragging and arrogance—only unadorned humility. Stunned Coca-Cola executives stepped up to the microphone and publicly apologized to the American people. They announced that the company would reissue the original Coca-Cola formula under a new name, Coke Classic.

Never before had a major corporation told the American people that it was sorry, never before had a corporate giant begged consumers for forgiveness—and never was an apology so quickly accepted.

But how could the company that owns the world's most famous trademark have been so wrong about its significance? How was a $7 billion corporation, which produces not just Coke but diet Coke, Tab, Sprite, Minute Maid orange juice, and movie hits like *Ghostbusters*, brought to its knees by consumers? Could Coca-Cola's management team, with its sterling track record, really have been so blind that it didn't foresee the fiasco? Or was the whole event a huge publicity stunt, a carefully calculated plot to launch a new cola and boost the sales of the old one?

The Real Coke, The Real Story is a behind-the-scenes account of how and why the company changed the taste of its flagship brand. Much of the story has never been told before. It involves the life of the Coca-Cola Company itself, from its early boom years, through a period of benign neglect and increasing losses to its major competitor, to the resurrection of the company under a new management in 1980. The Coca-Cola Company of the early 1980s was one of the most admired business organizations in the United States, according to a *Fortune* magazine poll of eight thousand business executives and analysts. It purchased Columbia Pictures Industries, formed Tri-Star Pictures, introduced diet Coke and cherry Coke, all the while increasing shareholders' return on investment by 22 percent. It seemed the management of Coca-Cola could do no wrong—just a moment before it made what appeared to be one of the major blunders in the chronicle of American business.

The result of that mistake is another part of the story—the remarkable reaction of those who refused to accept the axiom that the consumer is powerless in the face of a corporate giant and who persuaded Coca-Cola to bring back America's old friend.

CHAPTER 1

THEY DON'T MAKE COKE ANYMORE

The Coca-Cola Company's news of April 23, 1985, sent shock
waves across America. The unique taste of Coke would soon
be a thing of the past, no more than a memory evoking a different era, a different way of life. Some people cried, some
scoffed, some wrote scathing articles, and others frantically set
about to stockpile enormous hoards of their irreplaceable longtime favorite. But everywhere Coke's large and loyal following
asked, "Why did they do this to Coke?"

Dan Lauck, a reporter on KHLO-TV in San Antonio, Texas,
drinks little else but Coke—no beer, no coffee, no tea or milk.
Although he may have a mixed drink three or four times a year,
he never mixes Coke with alcohol—"Why ruin a good Coke?"
he asks. The thirty-five-year-old insists on drinking only Coke
that comes in the original six-and-a-half-ounce bottle, and his
habit, which has gone on since his college years, is to consume
twelve of these bottles a day. If he plays tennis in the hot Texas

sun, he may drink a whole case in a single day. To compensate for his immense caloric intake from Coke, Dan has had to forgo both breakfast and lunch.

Everywhere he goes, Dan carries a hand-held cooler. If he finds himself in a restaurant that doesn't serve the real thing, he'll bring in one Coke at a time from the ample supply in his VW convertible. And when he and his wife, Meg, go to a movie theater that serves a cola other than Coke, Meg lugs along an insulated pocketbook that is really a camouflaged cooler packed with bottles of Coke.

Dan will do just about anything to maintain his habit. At one time he was living and working in New York and the local Coca-Cola bottler stopped producing Coke in six-and-a-half-ounce bottles, so for five or six years Dan periodically drove all the way to Wilmington, Delaware, to buy his stash. Once he rented a truck and brought back 150 cases.

When Dan arrived at work on April 23, a day that Cokaholics have dubbed Black Tuesday, his managing editor asked if he felt as if his life had just gone down the toilet. Dan didn't know what she was talking about and didn't believe her when she told him that they were changing the taste of Coke. He called the Coca-Cola Company in Atlanta, and the people there confirmed what the world was just beginning to learn.

"I couldn't have been more surprised if someone had told me that I was gay," said the husband and father of two. "I was flabbergasted, and after twenty minutes in the funk, I asked our director if I could borrow his pickup truck." Dan drove to the San Antonio bottler and purchased 110 cases for $979.00. The next day he was torn between feeling guilty about spending so much money and wanting to stockpile even more Coke.

"I thought about cashing in some of my wife's stocks and buying more," he said.

Libby Lavine is a short, auburn-haired woman who gets teary-eyed when she hears the old Coke song "I'd like to teach the world to sing, in perfect harmony; I'd like to buy the world a Coke, and keep it company." In the basement of her comfortable home in Birmingham, Michigan, stands an old Coke vending machine stocked with ten-ounce bottles. Libby's kitchen telephone is shaped like a Coke bottle, with the push button numbers located under the base. Nearby is a transistor radio shaped like a modern-day Coca-Cola vending machine. Using all the discipline she can muster, Libby restricts herself to three ten-ounce bottles a day.

When Libby Lavine heard the Coca-Cola Company's news, she not only rushed out and bought $700 worth of Coke, she also got angry. She called the *Daily Tribune* in nearby Royal Oaks and placed a classified ad asking for letters from other old-Coke fans. A *Daily Trib* reporter picked up the story about her letter-writing campaign, and Libby was so swamped with mail that she rented a post office box to receive the letters. Within the first three days she got one hundred, and there would be many, many more.

Black Tuesday caught John Coit, a *Rocky Mountain News* columnist in Denver, hard-up for a story. Coit was a Vietnam veteran from South Carolina who had joined the *News* only a few years before. He was plugging along, trying to find a niche as a personal columnist in a strange town, a southern boy trying to tap into the sensitivities of the West. That day he happened to be walking past a newspaper street rack when he saw the *USA Today* headline about Coca-Cola changing its formula: "Sweeter Taste to Woo Pepsi Generation."

"I reacted as a consumer, not a columnist, and I was outraged," said Coit, a thirty-eight-year-old Coke enthusiast. But at least he had his topic for the day, and he sat down to write the first of what would be six columns about new Coke. First, he good-naturedly warned Coca-Cola that it had better not start pushing some "sugar-plum fairy gag juice" on the populace in place of "daddy juice," as some kids called the drink their fathers loved. And he ended the column with the kicker "The new stuff better be good." Like many journalists who initially wrote about new Coke, Coit had not yet tasted it, but that was beside the point—he didn't like the idea, period.

The Denver Coca-Cola Bottling Company was quick to respond to Coit's article. They sent him a whole case of new Coke with a promise that he would like the new taste.

"It was awful—worse than I imagined," recalled John. "I wondered who they had tested it on." And the headline of his second column blasted, "If IT Is Awful, Lousy, Then New Coke Is It." Among the many criticisms John leveled at new Coke was that it "tastes like a lousy imitation of Pepsi," and he predicted the stuff would fail.

Coit's protest against new Coke became a crusade, and he became the talk of the town, appearing on all the local TV and radio shows as the "mouse that roared." The subject of Coca-Cola proved to be very close to the hearts of many Denverites, earning Coit a new and faithful following for his column.*

---

* Coit died of a heart attack on January 2, 1986.

*　*　*

In Brookings, South Dakota, Duane Larson, the owner of Nick's Hamburgers, heard the news in his living room the night of Black Tuesday. He couldn't believe it and he didn't like it. A feisty, stubborn man, Duane had recently threatened the local Coca-Cola distributor that he might change to Pepsi because the last delivery of Coke (the original) had tasted flat.

Duane sponsored a softball team called Nick's and Coke, which had won the town championship a few years back. He always took Coke along when he went pheasant hunting, and he displayed a collection of Coke bottles in his hamburger shop on Main Street.

Two weeks after the news broke, Duane brought home his first can of new Coke, poured it over ice, waited a minute for it to get cold, and then took a swallow. When he told his wife it tasted lousy, she accused him of having been biased from day one. "You've been down on them since the announcement," Julie Larson said. So he shoved the glass of new Coke over to her and she took a sip. "You'd better call Pepsi," she said.

Like many vitriolic protestors against new Coke, Duane became something of a celebrity. A photo of him pouring a liter of new Coke out into the street appeared in the local paper. The *New York Times* called and interviewed him, and he was quoted in *Newsweek* magazine.

On April 23 a novelty song writer and singer named George Pickard turned on the midday news in Shoney's Inn in Nashville, Tennessee. When he heard the announcement about new Coke he reacted instantly. He put aside the album he was in Nashville to record for Wayne Hodge's Stargem Records and, within forty-five minutes, wrote some lyrics for a new song called "Coke *Was* It." He convinced Hodge to make a quick cut of the ballad, and the two worked the rest of the afternoon perfecting the lyrics.

Early the following morning Hodge had six musicians and three background singers ready to go. "Coke Was It" was recorded by noon, mixed and ready for stamping by six that Wednesday evening. The next day five thousand copies were pressed and sent to most of the nation's radio stations. Another two thousand would be pressed in May.

Pickard estimated that "Coke Was It" was played on the radio between three hundred thousand and four hundred thousand times. In addition, the TV program *20/20* and several local TV stations around the country broadcast the song. Even Coca-Cola headquarters itself apparently wanted the record. Roberto Goizueta, the chairman, got his own personal copy of "Coke Was It" and one hundred others were distributed throughout the rest of the company.

Consumers felt they had been excluded from the marketing mainstream of America. Their likes and passions obviously did not count; they were expected to be passive recipients of whatever the corporate world decided to give them. But, as it turned out, the public did not so easily relinquish Coke, nor did they want it to be improved. As one native of Atlanta remarked, "I don't think there's anything you could do to make it better. It's perfect."

CHAPTER 2

HOW IT ALL BEGAN

Although consumers of Coca-Cola felt like puppets in the hands of a whimsical puppeteer, the Coca-Cola Company did not come to its radical decision easily or quickly. How could it, without good cause, have tampered with the taste of a drink that was distributed to 155 countries and consumed more than 303 million times a day? Indeed, years of planning preceded the arrival of new Coke and years of internal problems contributed to the demise of the old one. Some of the seeds of those problems were in fact planted in the original formation of the Coca-Cola Company but would go unnoticed during the company's exciting boom years.

The taste of Coke, which became so much a part of American life, dates back over a century. In 1885, John Pemberton, an Atlanta pharmacist, registered a trademark for "French Wine Cola—Ideal Nerve and Tonic Stimulant," a brew he had developed in a three-legged pot he apparently stirred with an oar.

The name was appropriate, since the stimulant is said to have contained cocaine, along with wine and a few other ingredients. After about a year, Pemberton decided to change the formula; he removed the wine and added caffeine and, for flavor, extract of kola nut. At that point, his partner and bookkeeper, Frank Robinson, changed the name to Coca-Cola because he thought the two Cs, written in the Spencerian script that was popular at the time, would look good in advertising. Coca-Cola, which joined the ranks of the many mysterious potions being peddled by traveling salesmen, was sold as a cure for both hangovers and headaches.

Georgia businessman Asa Candler bought the [sole] rights to Coca-Cola from John Pemberton in 1889. To expand the business Candler began to sell Coca-Cola syrup to wholesalers, who in turn sold it to drugstores. There it was mixed with carbonated water and served at soda fountains. Candler also dreamed up the idea of serving Coke in the shapely little glasses that are now collectibles, and he sold these to wholesalers as well.

In 1889, Benjamin F. Thomas and Joseph P. Whitehead of Chattanooga, Tennessee, approached Candler with a proposition to bottle Coca-Cola. The two men are said to have thought of this merchandising scheme while they were in Cuba, where they noticed a beverage of some sort being consumed from bottles. Candler believed that sales of his drink would remain predominantly in the drugstore, and bottling was such an expensive operation that he wanted no part of it. Still, he saw the advantage of distributing his syrup to new markets, and he obliged the businessmen by selling them the right to bottle Coke throughout nearly all of the United States. The price was one dollar—possibly the steal of the century.

Thomas and Whitehead, assisted by financier John T. Lupton, promptly sold regional bottling rights to other businessmen in the South and later in the rest of the country. They created a network of independent bottlers numbering about one thousand by 1930. Each bottler had an exclusive right *in perpetuity* to bottle Coke in his area, and no one else except the soda fountains could sell Coke in that market. The bottlers actually owned the Coca-Cola trademark in their territories and the company could not refuse to sell them syrup. This setup, which formed the heart and soul of Coca-Cola's system, would come under attack nearly a century later when the Federal Trade Commission charged the company with violating antitrust laws by restricting competition.

Candler's budding Coca-Cola company did well enough to sell for $25 million in 1919, in what was the largest financial transaction to date in the South. The purchaser was entrepreneur Ernest Woodruff, president of the Commercial Travelers Savings Bank, later the Trust Company of Georgia, whose vaults still guard the recipe for Coke. Woodruff was head of a syndicate of investors who had helped build not only one of the state's largest banks but also the Atlantic Ice and Coal Company, the Atlantic Steel Company, and the Continental Gin Company. But Woodruff was in business for more than just the money. Hard work, to the exclusion of almost everything else, was his raison d'être, and he assumed that that principle applied to his family as well. Legend has it that when the board of directors of Atlantic Ice and Coal recommended a raise for his son, Robert, Ernest entered a resounding veto, and Robert quit.

Despite Woodruff's unflagging commitment, Coca-Cola fizzled in the early twenties. Sales of Coke syrup dropped from 18.7 million gallons in 1918 to 15.4 million gallons in 1922, and the price of Coca-Cola stock plummeted from $40 to $18 in the same years. Profits fell primarily because the company's cost of syrup skyrocketed while its cost to the bottlers stayed the same. Back in 1899 Candler had contracted with his bottlers to sell them syrup at a fixed price, and that contract was still binding. In Candler's day sugar, a key ingredient, cost only seven cents a pound, but by the time Ernest Woodruff was in charge of things, postwar inflation had quadrupled that figure. When the staggering company tried to pass on some of the burden to the bottlers, they sued.

In 1921 the opponents agreed to a decree that fixed the price of syrup at the 1921 current price, subject to quarterly adjustments based on the price of sugar. Thus the costs of all the ingredients in the syrup *except sugar* were locked at the 1921 level. The bottlers had to pick up any fluctuations in sugar price, paying whatever Coke had to pay for it. Woodruff may have been farsighted—the agreement worked fine for fifty years—but even he could not have forecast the wildfire inflation of the seventies, when spiraling costs of the other syrup ingredients would make it scarcely possible for the company to make a profit on Coke.

Swamped with legal battles against its many imitators, threatened by bankruptcy, the 1920s Coca-Cola Company was at an impasse. To restore morale as well as profits, the board of directors turned to a new generation. Robert Winship Woodruff, thirty-three, was then pulling in a hefty $85,000 a year as general manager of White Motor, a truck company in Cleveland, Ohio. In April 1923, Robert became president of Coca-Cola.

The Boss, as he came to be called, would make the name Coke virtually synonymous with that of America around the world. Yet this dominant figure worked behind the scenes in relative anonymity. He hired a public relations man to keep his name *out* of the newspapers and told the publisher of *The Atlanta Constitution* that he didn't want to see his name in that paper again unless he was convicted of rape. A plaque on his desk read, "There is no limit to what a man can do or where he can go if he doesn't mind who gets the credit," a saying that perhaps no other corporate president before or since has endorsed. With his fedora, and a cigar permanently jutting from his teeth, he led the company through the strength of his personality.

Robert's leadership and financial skills had blossomed early. At the Georgia Military Academy near Atlanta he managed the school newspaper, the football team, and the drama club, and raised funds to start a school band. Academic subjects played a secondary role at best. Robert didn't see the need for a formal education—he knew he was going to be a businessman and he wanted to get out and start making money. So in 1909, after only a year at Emory College at Oxford near Atlanta, he defied his father's orders and left school for the world of business. Restless and relentlessly ambitious, he hopped quickly from the job of apprentice machinist at the General Pipe and Foundry Company (where he worked for sixty cents a day), to that of salesman at Atlanta's Fire Extinguisher Company, to the position of purchasing agent for Atlanta Ice and Coal. Leaving the family businesses behind, he went to White Motor, where he became vice-president as well as general manager.

The Boss was a stocky, gruff, and strong-willed man who did things his own way from an early age. As soon as he got to the troubled Coca-Cola Company, he launched radical new programs, insisting on quality control and firing-up the bottling industry to help make his product ubiquitous. These strategies may seem obvious to a generation raised on soft drinks, but in Woodruff's day they signaled singular foresight and acumen. He seemed to know instinctively what was right for Coca-Cola.

Early in his reign Woodruff called a meeting of his sales force and, without warning, announced to the shocked members of the audience that they were fired. The company had eliminated the sales department, he said. The next day he called back the stunned employees and rehired them for his new "service" department. Now they were called "servicemen," and selling Coke syrup was only part of their job. At the soda fountains, they would help install new machinery, train retailers to dispense syrup properly, and find better methods of mixing the peppy drink. At the bottling plants, servicemen would increase productivity and efficiency by advising on all aspects of the operation, from machinery to shipping. With Woodruff's sweeping quality-control programs now under way, Coke enthusiasts· could expect to find one and only one unmistakable Coke taste in the North and in the South, from coast to coast.

Placing Coke "within arm's reach of desire" anywhere and everywhere in the country was another of Woodruff's ambitions. Why not make it available at gas stations, factories, office buildings, movie theaters, baseball parks, even churches?

Wherever there are people who get thirsty, make Coke an option. Woodruff realized the enormous potential of the bottle as a means to carry out his dream. Coke in bottles could go anywhere, be sold anywhere, and be consumed anywhere. If people sipped Coke at the drugstore soda fountain and then saw bottles on the grocery-store shelf, they'd probably buy it.

Within Woodruff's first five years at the helm, Coca-Cola in bottles began to outsell Coke sold at the soda fountains. Coke cropped up, as the 1927 advertising slogan claimed, "around the corner from anywhere." Today some observers hypothesize that Pepsi eventually caught up with Coke not because of inventive advertising or a better taste but because Pepsi finally became as ubiquitous as its rival. In the 1980s soft drinks became so widespread they overtook tap water as the number-one beverage in the United States.

When Woodruff took control, Coca-Cola had trickled into Canada, Cuba, and Puerto Rico but otherwise was unknown around the world. Curious about its potential to please the foreign palate, Woodruff outlined a plan in 1926 to test the drink in Europe. When the board of directors balked, he proceeded in secrecy, establishing a foreign sales department and showing a profit within three years. Only then did he inform the directors of his disobedience. Spreading Coke around the world was the feat Woodruff was proudest of, yet he remained unassuming and reluctant to give himself too much credit. "I didn't have vision," he remarked. "I was just curious."

Yes, Woodruff was persistently curious, but he was stubborn, too, and in marketing Coke abroad, he again stood up to the executives. Once it was clear the drink would be sold overseas, there were those who recommended modifying its flavor to suit the taste buds of each nationality. But Woodruff stuck to his belief in the universal appeal of Coke's single, secret formula.

During World War II Coke deluged the globe. Wherever the GIs went, there went Coke. "See that every man in uniform gets a bottle of Coca-Cola for five cents wherever he is and whatever it costs the company," Woodruff ordered his staff in 1941. Considered a morale booster and emblem of home for the homesick soldier, Coke's catchy new slogans like "It's the real thing" and "The global high sign" spoke to the GIs far afield, and they responded with unequivocal enthusiasm. In the course of the war, they drank five billion bottles of Coke.

Initially the popular drink was shipped to the armed forces in bottles from a base in Iceland, but this method became cumbersome as demand increased. In 1943 General Dwight Eisenhower in the Allied headquarters in North Africa requested that the War Department establish ten bottling plants, in Morocco, Cairo, Casablanca, and elsewhere in North Africa, and also in Italy. The War Department provided the machinery and personnel—usually soldiers who had worked for Coca-Cola prior to the war—and wherever necessary Coca-Cola sent civilian company-employed "technical observers." By the end of the war there were sixty-four bottling plants worldwide, built at government expense; these the company then incorporated—without cost.

At the headquarters in Atlanta, meanwhile, there had been some shifting of seats, though in essence Woodruff continued to hold the reins. In 1939 he had "retired" as president, but he acted as chairman of the board until 1942, at which point he became chairman of the board's executive committee. In 1954, at the age of sixty-five, he "officially retired" again, this time moving to another office and holding a position specially created for him. As chairman of the finance committee he essentially controlled the purse strings of the company, since no one could spend more than $100,000 without the approval of his committee.

What was the company's financial situation in the fifties? Coca-Cola ruled the soft-drink world, and its name was as universally known as that of any other product in commercial history. Sales were $144.7 million in 1955, bringing in net profits of $27.5 million. Woodruff was not one to skimp when it came to telling the world about Coca-Cola: the advertising budget was $30 million that year. Talented artists like Norman Rockwell and Haddon Sundblom created masterly four-color illustrations. Billboard advertisements abounded. Radio and TV intoned, "What you need is a Coke."

No other soft drink could touch Coca-Cola in the fifties. The favorite outsold its nearest rival, Pepsi-Cola, by better than two to one. In the early thirties Pepsi-Cola had, in fact, faced bankruptcy and Woodruff could have bought the company for a nominal fee. He declined on the grounds that it wouldn't be helpful to market a drink that would compete with Coke. Had Woodruff had a crystal ball showing scenes from the seventies, he would probably have leaped at the chance to eliminate what would become Coke's fiercest competitor.

Woodruff had become a man of vast wealth. He owned five houses, his favorite being the rural Ichauway, a 30,000-acre plantation in southern Georgia. Even in the 1980s this sprawling retreat with its white clapboard houses, stables, kennels, and servants' quarters retained a distinctive old-fashioned flavor, described by John Huey of the *Wall Street Journal*:

> This place and its people are of another time. Matched pairs of mules hitched in brass-studded harness still haul dog wagons with leather benches to the hunt. Black servants in crisp white smocks serve lunches of dove pie with nutmeg, corn pancakes sopped in sorghum syrup, and cold home-churned buttermilk in figurined ceramic mugs. Afterwards, they stoop to offer moist Havana cigars from fine-grained humidors.

At Ichauway, which means "where many deer sleep," Woodruff relaxed, contemplated business decisions, and hunted. He also maintained a mansion in Atlanta and a River House apartment in New York City at Fifty-second Street on the East River. He acquired a small place in Wilmington, Delaware, because in 1933 he had moved the entire corporate headquarters to that city to avoid a new Georgia state tax on corporate properties and securities. Only when the onerous tax was repealed in 1946 did Woodruff return his company to Atlanta. Last, he owned a 4,600-acre horse-and-cattle ranch in Wyoming, once the homestead of William ("Buffalo Bill") Cody.

Woodruff's real-estate holdings seemed a bit excessive to his more puritanical father, but when Ernest Woodruff complained about the number of houses he owned, Robert replied, "Yes, but I'm probably the only fella you know with the same wife in all of them." Woodruff had been married to Nell Hodgson since 1912. The two never had children but he and Nell remained happily together until her death in 1968. "It has never been my desire," he confessed, "to have a yacht, a racehorse or mistress—in that order."

Nor, apparently, did he ever read a book or listen to music or look at art, with the exception of wildlife painting. Robert had inherited his father's work ethic, and according to Joseph W. Jones, his personal secretary for nearly forty years, he had trouble admitting ever having a good time. He did, however, entertain at his plantation people like President Dwight Eisenhower and the golfer Bobby Jones, with whom he founded the Augusta National Golf Club and the Masters Tournament.

A multimillionaire, Robert Woodruff spent relatively modestly and had quantities of cash to spare. With a personal fortune estimated at the time of his death in 1985 at over a quarter of a billion dollars, he was one of the world's greatest philanthropists, donating an estimated $350 million to benefit medicine, education, and the arts. In this sphere, too, Woodruff had his own way of doing things—just as he wished to keep his corporate life out of the limelight, so he made his gifts anonymously until the last few years of his life. "Mr. Anonymous," as he was sometimes called in Atlanta, gave $225 million to Emory University. The Atlanta Art Center Alliance, which includes a museum, symphony hall, theater, and arts college, received a generous $28 million from Woodruff and was renamed for him in 1982. He gave three parks to the city and made possible, through his political influence and the donation of land, the establishment of the National Centers for Disease Control in Atlanta. Add to this legacy the national attention brought to the city by the Coca-Cola Company, and one can say that Woodruff in essence made his hometown the capital of the South.

Obviously, the king of Coca-Cola had influence with politicians in Atlanta, but he was also well-connected in Washington.

When the federal government ordered Atlanta's public schools integrated in 1961 and officials were threatening to close the schools rather than comply, Woodruff advocated keeping them open at all costs. Coca-Cola's counsel and director, John A. Sibley, led statewide hearings on the issue that helped lead the way toward integration.

Woodruff's liberal political voice was heard in 1968, too, when Martin Luther King, Jr., was killed. Woodruff was in the White House at the time and was informed of King's death by Lyndon Johnson. Woodruff called Atlanta's mayor, Ivan Allen, Jr., and pledged to underwrite any additional costs to the city to make sure that King's hometown remained orderly and paid proper respect to the slain civil rights leader.

Throughout the fifties and sixties the sailing was smooth for Coca-Cola, and Woodruff in effect remained at the tiller through the seventies. According to Jones, not a single recommendation from the Boss was voted down during those years. In fact, board meetings were adjourned for lack of a quorum if "the man with the cigar" had been detained somewhere. The Boss always had a hand in choosing the chief executive officer, and his philosophy—"support the management or change the management"—made itself felt. To Woodruff, management meant the chairman's office. So even presidents of Coca-Cola as well liked by Woodruff as Charles Duncan and Lucian Smith, when they fought with Chairman J. Paul Austin in the seventies, lost the battle and resigned.

The sixties were a time of diversification and expansion at Coca-Cola. The company bought the Minute Maid Corporation, a top-ranking frozen-foods business, and the Duncan Foods Corporation, which together became the Coca-Cola

Foods Division, best known for products like Minute Maid orange juice, Hi-C, and Butternut Coffee. Sprite was introduced by the company in 1961. Tab, introduced in 1963, was the leading diet soda until the arrival of diet Coke nearly two decades later. Sales exceeded $1 billion in 1967, reaping profits of $100 million. And in 1969 Coca-Cola's advertising agency, McCann-Erickson, revived the classic 1942 slogan "It's the real thing." Set to a wonderful melody, it became an advertising sensation equal to Wendy's "Where's the beef?" and the winning slogan of Coke's rival, "We're the Pepsi Generation."

All told, to the Coca-Cola executives of the sixties, the future looked bright. Everyone connected with Coca-Cola was making money. The policies of the past decades that would soon rock the company had not yet revealed themselves.

CHAPTER 3

TROUBLE IN ATLANTA

To the world that watched upbeat Coke ads, packed Coke for every picnic, and stocked Coke for every party, the Coca-Cola Company appeared huge and healthy throughout the seventies. But behind the scenes, executives were ensnared in a very different drama, bickering among themselves, distracted by tangential issues, and losing sight of the heart of the matter—Coke itself. The top executives of the Coca-Cola Company of the late seventies actually paid less and less attention to the marketing and sale of their central product, so caught up were they in dodging government allegations, fighting with bottlers over the price of syrup, and squabbling over whether or not to control who owned the company franchises. Gone were the days of the inspired entrepreneur and the spritely intellect, gone the days of unswerving leadership.

The FTC opened fire on Coca-Cola in 1971, charging that the bottlers' contracts granting territorial exclusivity restricted competition. If the government prevailed, anyone, including a bigger, richer bottler, could invade a bottler's territory and take a substantial if not fatal bite out of his market. This "walls down" world, as the concept was called at Coca-Cola headquarters, would make a bottler's future quite uncertain and would therefore reduce the value of his franchise. It could result in anarchy, and it was horrifying to all except Coca-Cola's expansionist bottlers, who foresaw an opportunity to widen their domains. So anxious was Robert Woodruff over the impending change that he told Coca-Cola's president, Lucian Smith, he would preserve the status quo even if he, Woodruff, had to commit his personal fortune to the cause. The obsessiveness of the patriarch fairly hypnotized the company.

"Our system was immobilized," said Donald R. Keough, who, as president of the company's domestic soft-drink unit, Coca-Cola USA, found himself in the thick of it. It is astounding to imagine it now, but the first *fifty* meetings he attended after assuming office in 1974 were legal briefings on the FTC battle. "I was practicing law," said Keough, who is a consummate salesman and former president of the Coca-Cola Foods Division but is not a lawyer. "Looking back, I made a mistake. I should have hired a roomful of lawyers and told them to deal with it and we could have gotten on with the business."

In October 1975, an administrative law judge ruled that the Coca-Cola bottlers' territorial exclusivity was not a violation of federal trade regulations, but two and a half years later the judge's ruling was reversed and the FTC reinstituted its complaint. By 1978 little else was talked about at company headquarters and, said one senior executive, "After hearing discussion after discussion of the 'walls down' possibility, you

felt too despondent to get on with business." Keough confessed
that long-range planning was thwarted, too. "We always had
to confront the reality that the system as we knew it might not
exist, and we were painting the worst-case scenario." So obsessed was everyone with the FTC that they forgot the essence
of what they were fighting for—the right to sell Coke, with the
emphasis on "sell." The battle was to last a decade, ten years
in which officials admit the company took its eye off the ball
while its rival, Pepsi, kept its own cola sharply in focus. With
its image rejuvenated by the "Pepsi Generation" campaign and
the product itself more generally available, Pepsi-Cola in 1975
pulled ahead of Coca-Cola in supermarket sales.

There was another conflict closer at hand, within the very
walls of the Atlanta headquarters. Eventually disputes with
bottlers over the problem of escalating syrup costs would pit
both Keough and Chairman J. Paul Austin against Lucian
Smith, the company president and chief operating officer.

The hyperinflation of the 1970s sent the price of syrup ingredients skyrocketing far beyond anything Ernest Woodruff had
foreseen when he signed the bottlers' contract in 1921. As we've
seen, that agreement allowed for sugar-price fluctuation but
not for a rise in the price of the other Coke ingredients. By
1976 insiders at Coca-Cola could easily envision a time when,
if the economy continued its course, it would cost the company
more to produce Coke syrup than the bottlers paid for it. Their
only recourse was to induce the bottlers to amend their contracts to allow for a flexible price that would reflect future
inflation. In exchange, the company promised that it would
spend more on marketing. Luke Smith, who spearheaded the
move, was a well-liked, affable, though aggressive, character,

but he met his match in this debate—first in the bottlers, ulti-
mately in Keough. The bottlers put up such fierce and pro-
longed resistance to any price change that the business maneu-
vers came to resemble a family feud. "Every bottler on his
dying bed calls his son to his side and, speaking his last words,
says 'Don't you ever let them mess with that contract,'" said
Keough. It was like trying to talk someone out of a birthright.

The bottlers who opposed the amendment found a powerful
champion in the chairman of the New York Coca-Cola Bottling
Company, Charles Millard. The lean tall man with light blue
eyes and graying hair was used to getting his way. He agreed
that some accommodation was necessary but he wanted an
annual cap on how much the company could raise the price of
syrup. His opposition was immensely effective because, until
bottlers representing 50 percent of the company's domestic
volume agreed to the amendment, its provisions could not take
effect. As long as Millard and the large bottlers who supported
him held out, Coca-Cola would have to continue selling syrup
at 1921 prices. Other bottlers acknowledged that this outdated
price was illogical, and Luke Smith was amassing such forces
in his camp. John Lupton—the scion and namesake of the
original Chattanooga, Tennessee, bottler, a member of the
board of directors, and the world's largest and wealthiest bottler—had agreed to the amendment. Smith, a master salesman,
had convinced many smaller bottlers to accept the amendment
on faith, and in 1978 he was tangling with the larger bottlers
in New York, Los Angeles, and Florida. According to Millard,
"It became a crusade for Luke, and he became messianic."

The amendment process caused a lot of resentment among
the bottlers, and some telling remarks surfaced about how

business was run at Coca-Cola. One Georgia bottler harangued Smith: "You've got some arrogant sumbitches in Atlanta. You're a bureaucratic, nonresponsive bunch down there. It takes six days to get somebody to return our phone calls."

By mid-1978 the amendment process was at an impasse, and Millard, who could no longer deal with Smith, went around him to Keough. This move put Keough in an awkward position, since Smith, the point man in the amendment process as well as the company president, was clearly his superior. But to get business back on track he sided with Millard. Keough, a self-made man who is the son of a third-generation Irish cattleman, is a persuasive executive with impeccable manners. He convinced Austin and Woodruff of the necessity of the cap on syrup prices. Within ninety days the Coca-Cola Company, with the approval of the board of directors, agreed.

"It was a blow to Luke's ego," said Millard, "and that was the beginning of the end for Luke." His relationship with Chairman Austin became strained to the point that the two highest-ranking officers of the Coca-Cola Company didn't speak to each other—hardly a productive climate for business. Furthermore, because Smith had been preoccupied with the syrup amendment at the expense of day-to-day business, in 1978 Austin established an Office of the Chairman, consisting of seven executive vice-presidents. They were in essence to assume Smith's duties as chief operating officer. Slighted by the blatant reduction of his role, Smith resigned from the company a year later.

At Keough's side in his dispute with Smith was a tall, ruddy-faced, high-strung Argentinian named Brian Dyson. Keough had lured Dyson to the main office in 1978 to head up the USA division when he himself was promoted to the top post for both North and South American operations. Dyson, aware of the mess the company was in and concerned about how U.S. bottlers would respond to a foreigner, had been reluctant to take the job. "I wasn't looking at the USA division as a great opportunity, but the principle was that if the company asked you to do something, you should."

The new president of Coca-Cola USA was not lacking in ideas and the energy to see them through. He would pace his office while talking, stopping now and then and close his eyes in concentration, or sit, leaning against his desk, like a cat ready to pounce. His first target was the company's laissez-faire attitude toward changes in bottling-franchise ownerships. "I was deeply surprised that the company seemed to shy away from trying to manage change," Dyson commented. "I was surprised we were not helping to change bottlers or going after bad ones and saying, this can't be good for you, let us buy you out." Yet under the existing system, if a bottler decided to sell, the company couldn't stop him from transferring the contract to a new owner, who then attained all rights in perpetuity, including the right to purchase syrup from Coca-Cola and the right to sell the contract to whomever he pleased. Under this system, the company had no real control over who was selling its products, or how well, or for how long. According to Chairman Austin, it simply wasn't company policy to get involved with franchise transfers. But Dyson found a zealous supporter in Keough, who had arrived at the same conclusion.

The hazards of this system were terrifying during the amendment debate, when it became clear that a bottler who would not agree to the amendment could sell his franchise to like-minded businessmen or buy other franchises himself. It was in the company's interests to keep the franchises in the hands of the pro-amendment bottlers and restrict the growth of the non-amenders, but the loose system prevented that control. Before Keough and Dyson agreed to compromise with Millard, the Washington, D.C., franchise came up for sale, and the two executives blocked a prominent suitor, Northwest Industries, solely because it was an antiamendment bottler.

More important, Keough and Dyson saw that the company's lack of control had led over the years to mismanagement and lost income. Too many of the franchises were in the hands of third-generation owners who were more concerned about paying Aunt Mildred her quarterly dividend check than about investing in the business. If Coke had a very high market share in a particular territory, for example, an owner could sacrifice a few of those share points to increase his near-term profits. Better known as milking the franchise, this practice eventually leads to outdated equipment and, worse, a weak bottler unable to stem the decline in market share. Keough said the company worried that certain owners were milking the business by cutting capital spending, using such methods as running old trucks into the ground rather than replacing them. "You'll lose share," Keough said, "but in the meantime, you can draw out a lot of cash."

In their battle to change the inefficient system, Dyson and Keough had to come up with a strategy that would sway Paul Austin. The chairman was nearing the end of his reign and his governing philosophy was to preserve the kingdom he had overseen—as president, then as chief executive officer, and then as chairman of the board—for nearly two decades. Finally,

Dyson hit upon the irrefutable argument that the Coca-Cola Company should have a say in franchise ownership since these owners' performances determined the company's performance. Austin couldn't argue with that.

In 1979 he and the board approved a deal structured by Keough and Dyson for the sale of the Washington, D.C., franchise. It resulted in the first of the company's many leveraged buyouts, now one of Wall Street's favorite tactics for acquisitions and takeovers. In a leveraged buyout, the buyers borrow most of the purchase price, using the assets of the acquired company as collateral. For their first deal, Coca-Cola got the managers of the D.C. franchise together with Citicorp and Prudential, and the joined forces became known as Mid-Atlantic. This new company bought the D.C. franchise from its owner, James E. Krass. At the same time they also bought the Baltimore franchise, which was owned by the Coca-Cola Company itself. The Coca-Cola Company pitched in by loaning the buyers $47 million. The deal kept the new franchise out of unfriendly hands and, more important, showed the board that this could be done without undue cost to the company.

According to Dyson's strategy, each time a franchise came up for sale, Coca-Cola would either find a buyer or purchase the franchise itself and resell it. This method would also allow it to organize regional companies into larger distributorships that made more sense geographically. The balance of public versus private ownership could be influenced from Atlanta. Dyson reasoned that private companies could, if necessary, sacrifice immediate gains for long-term beneficial business improvements, while a public company is subject to short-term pressure from shareholders and analysts. With the value of private ownership in mind, Coca-Cola purchased 9.5 percent of the publicly held Coca-Cola Bottling Company of New York for $15 million in 1979. It was the beginning of a $250 million leveraged buyout process that would take a year and a half to complete and would make the largest Coca-Cola bottling company a privately held company. At the same time Coca-Cola realized that company-owned bottlers presented a handsome profit center for the corporation. It bought the Atlanta Coca-Cola Bottling Company for $65 million in 1979, and in the following years an increasing number of franchises would come under the auspices of the mother company.

One can argue that all the dust raised by Dyson's restructuring program further obfuscated the problem of keeping Coke first in the public eye. One can argue that executives looked no farther than the company walls or at best to the bottling plants and the bottlers' gripes instead of at the marketplace and the competition. But, those executives would counter, the company *had* to assume more control, had to curb mismanagement, had to put franchises in competent, aggressive hands *in order* for business to pick up speed.

The FTC complaint was laid to rest once and for all in 1980 with a ruling in favor of the company. Once that happened, management knew the franchises would be worth a tremendous amount and that much changing of hands would follow. By the mid-eighties changes in ownership had occurred in franchises covering 53 percent of the U.S. population and accounting for half the company's volume. Each time a transaction occurred, Coca-Cola was involved, insisting on a transfer agreement that gives the company the first right of refusal if a franchise comes up for sale. Keough told every would-be buyer, "If you want this, you have to sign that agreement."

If Keough and Dyson made some inroads into the outdated systems at Coca-Cola, the prevailing atmosphere in the late seventies remained cloudy, lethargic, and unproductive. Managers spent all too many hours speculating over who would succeed the aging chairman of the board, and Austin himself contributed to the malaise by deciding to linger on a year past his designated 1980 retirement. The years 1978 to 1980 were "a two-year transition period," said Keough, "not unlike the transitions of governments, and the system came to a parade halt." Furthermore, under Austin's divisive Office of the Chairman setup with its multiple vice-chairmen, power was fractured and spread too thin—no one was really running the company.

The leadership seemed unable to keep pace with the changing times. Operating methods that had served the company in the boom years no longer worked. The oil embargo, inflation, and unprecedented interest rates in the seventies changed forever the way corporate America did business. The cultural climate was shifting too, with a strong effect on the soft-drink market. The baby-boomers who were coming of age valued ethnicity over the traditional ideal of the melting pot, diversity in people over similarity. For the "me generation" a single, universal product would no longer suffice. Baby-boomers demanded variety in their cars and clothes and their soft drinks. They might order a sugar cola at lunch, want a diet drink in the afternoon, and consider only a caffeine-free drink at night.

It was not the climate for an eighty-nine-year-old king and

his less-than-youthful board. In 1979 the average age of the directors on Coke's board was seventy. Only one of fourteen directors was under fifty, three were in their eighties, and one was over ninety. "One day Woodruff will die," said one senior executive to his wife in anticipation of a new era. But she calmly replied, "There are a lot of dead men who said that twenty years ago."

With Woodruff still at the helm, it was too easy for managers to forget that Coca-Cola was a public and not a private company and that they were responsible to the shareholders. In the second half of the seventies the compounded return on the Coca-Cola shareholders' investment was less than 1 percent. Small wonder the company had no desire to communicate with any shareholders other than the ones who sat on its board. In those years Coca-Cola officials, who, in accordance with Woodruff's wishes, had never been friendly with the news media, even stopped talking to securities analysts, the researchers who work for brokerage houses and who advise about the buying and selling of stocks. And when someone asked Woodruff himself if it was a good time to sell Coca-Cola stock, the perplexed boss replied, "I don't know. I've never sold any."

Return on capital was another useful guideline overlooked by the anachronistic managers, and Coca-Cola's fountain business was one—and not the only—victim of that oversight. The American fountain business is one of the company's more profitable ventures; it was the company's fountain sales that kept Coke the best-selling soft drink, even though since 1975 Pepsi had outsold it in grocery stores in every year except 1976. But the fountain business, which includes such customers as Mc-

Donald's and other fast-food chains that serve Coke in cups, had become more capital-intensive over the years, requiring more-sophisticated, expensive equipment. Apparently this detail escaped the notice of upper management until 1980, when an official finally discovered that the fountain business was generating only a 13 percent return on capital at a time when funds cost 14 percent. In theory, Coca-Cola was liquidating the business.

Coca-Cola made some blundering attempts at diversification in the seventies, too, but these attempts were seldom motivated by the prospect of making money. Instead, they were tailored to meet the personal needs of a few executives and to enhance their prestige. In 1970 Coca-Cola bought Aqua-Chem, Inc., which produces water-treatment equipment and industrial boilers. The reasoning was that this would be a tool for getting into the Arab countries, which refused to deal with Coca-Cola because the company did business with Israel. The Arabs needed Aqua-Chem technology. Coca-Cola would supply it, and robed Arabs would soon be sipping Coke. Initially Aqua-Chem was headed up by John Collings, an ambitious executive who would become the company's chief financial officer. But by the mid-seventies management whimsically decided that Aqua-Chem was too small an operation to suit Collings's talents. So in 1978 Coca-Cola bought Presto Products, a plastic-bag maker, and handed it to Collings. Add to this gift-giving the irony that Aqua-Chem failed on all counts, never earning enough to equal the dividends on the Coke shares with which the company bought it and never making an impact on the Arab boycott.

Forays into the wine industry didn't do any better. The Wine Spectrum, whose best-known label was Taylor California Cellars, was purchased in 1977. It made no money in three years, and the construction of a $35 million winery in Napa Valley would never bring about an adequate return on investment. In fact, the Wine Spectrum turned a meager profit only one year. Coca-Cola sold it in 1983 to Joseph E. Seagram & Sons, Inc. Hindsight in the 1980s says Coca-Cola never should have touched the wine business, but at the time no one considered how long it would take to recoup the ongoing investment; no one took stock of how tough the competition, Gallo, could be and how many millions of dollars it would take to put a new wine alongside Gallo brands. Coca-Cola's thinking was "A beverage is a beverage; if we did well with one, let's try another." That kind of strategy obviously couldn't keep a company on course in the turbulent tides of the seventies business world.

Not only were Coca-Cola's top-level managers paying no attention to return on investment, return on stockholders' equity, profit margins, and cost control, but their personnel decisions reflected the good-old-boys' regime. Managers' compensation was awarded "not on performance, but perfect attendance," said Keough. Who you knew was more important than how you performed, and arrogance permeated the company. A big bottler from outside the United States once told Keough that Coca-Cola's representative in that region would talk only to the president of the bottling company and wouldn't be bothered with anyone else. Keough was outraged and later informed the Coca-Cola executive that "if the janitor calls, you talk to him. We're not here for the business to serve us, we're here to serve the business."

Coca-Cola's complacency, haughtiness, and inability to change finally took their toll on the company's coffers. The growth rate of Coca-Cola's soft-drink volume between 1976 and 1979 dropped from 13 percent annually to a meager 2 percent. Profits between 1978 and 1981 grew at a compound annual rate of only 7 percent, and net income for 1980 increased a mere 0.5 percent. These hard, cold figures, sufficient to make insomniacs out of the best of managers, would be impossible to ignore in coming years. But for the moment, Coca-Cola remained a leviathan with atrophied muscles, and myopia, a company more comfortable in dreaming about the days when it ruled the world of soft drinks than in adapting to new times and a new marketplace. The system was so large and complex that it did not come to a halt, but it certainly spent those years faltering.

CHAPTER 4

THE CHALLENGE

All the while the Coca-Cola Company was absorbed in legal and internal battles, its arch-rival, Pepsi-Cola, had its eye on the main event. By staying alert to changing markets and advertising innovation, Pepsi-Cola was to come face to face with number one in full view of an amazed audience. First would come the "Pepsi Generation," an advertising campaign that captured the imagination of the baby-boomers with its idealism and youthful vigor. It enhanced not only the image of Pepsi-Cola but also that of anyone who chose to drink it.

Pepsi-Cola then would strike a blow that was to rock the king of colas. Though it didn't defeat Coke, it did shake the company's pride and confidence. As we will see, the "Pepsi Challenge" would present the results of comparative taste tests across America that showed a clear preference for Pepsi. While this news would not drastically change Coca-Cola's market share, the long-term effect was perhaps more devastating: the dumbfounded Coca-Cola Company, for the first time, would question the sacred, universally accepted taste of Coke.

The 1960s saw a wizard in charge of advertising at Pepsi-Cola. Alan Pottasch, a suave, well-tailored executive, completely revamped the company's advertising strategy. "In the 1960s we stopped talking about the product and started talking about the user, and that is a major difference," explained Pottasch. "We made cola into a necktie product. What you drank said something about who you were. We painted an image of our consumer as active, vital, and young at heart."

Once Pottasch had conceived the right consumer image, his job was to target a group whose taste buds weren't yet going steady with Coke, and to let that market know they had a choice when it came to colas. As he told *Adweek* magazine, "The word Coke had practically become generic. And that gave us the problem we've been chipping away at ever since. It forced us to position ourselves with those who had not yet developed this generic association. It forced us to look at the next generation of consumers as the only ones who might not have to rectify their behavior, their attitudes, toward colas." And that next generation just happened to be the baby-boomers, the postwar babies who would compose the largest single generation in our nation's history.

In 1963 that generation took on a new identity when Pottasch and his colleagues came up wtih the phrase "Pepsi Generation," one of the most enduring theme lines in American advertising history. From time to time an advertising idea transcends its slogans and jingles and becomes something more—a way of thinking, a way of life—and "Pepsi Generation" did just that. It entered the vernacular as a widely used figure of speech to define a certain group, and it therefore elevated Pepsi's image in many people's minds. It became acceptable to say "Pepsi, please." No longer was Pepsi the drink to gulp in the kitchen while Coke was being served in the living room.

In 1975 Pepsi's national advertising campaign was built around a new slogan, but the underlying concept of the "Pepsi Generation" was still there. The line "Join the Pepsi people, feelin' free" inspired upbeat commercials aimed at a populace anxious to recover from Vietnam, Watergate, and a severe economic recession. This warm, homey campaign with its dads and kids and fun and games used traditional Madison Avenue images to depict Pepsi's target audience. Their enthusiasm for life—and for Pepsi as an integral part of it—caught on in many parts of the country.

The South, however, remained Coke heartland, stubborn in its loyalty to its native drink. The job of cracking the market was assigned to a twenty-year Pepsi veteran named Larry Smith, who was himself from South Carolina. Smith arrived in Texas in 1975 to take over the direction of the Pepsi-owned bottling franchises in that state, where Coca-Cola commanded an overwhelming lead. "Texas was a disaster," recalled Smith, whose gentlemanly manner belies a tough managerial style. He'd been sent by Pepsi-Cola to convince Texans in the city of Dallas to give Pepsi a try, for not only did his brand trail Coke, it also lagged behind the home-brew Dr Pepper, which was number two among the cowboys and oil barons. Smith set off for this disaster zone with standard Pepsi marching orders: "Come back wearing your shield, or on it."

Smith's first move was to approach a major grocery chain in Dallas and offer to finance a Pepsi promotion. He told them that Pepsi would pay the chain a certain amount of money and sell Pepsi to them at a discount in exchange for the stores' promoting Pepsi in newspaper ads and prominent in-store displays. Smith's proposal barely got a hearing. "They said they didn't need us," Smith recalled. "Coke had a thirty-five share, Dr Pepper had a twenty-five, and Pepsi was an also-ran at six." Why should a chain store bother to promote such a minor brand? How many shoppers would be lured in by an also-ran?

To come up with a less conventional approach, Smith did a lot of thinking about the status of the two rival colas. He knew that in 1974 Pepsi nationwide had drawn even with Coke's sales in supermarkets, where people could choose from whatever was on the shelf. But owing to Coke's exclusive presence in fast-food chains such as McDonald's and Burger King, Coke held an overall commanding market share, which helped perpetuate the myth that Coke was far superior to Pepsi. That perception irked Smith, who felt sure that Pepsi was the better product. "We had a joke: if you put Coke in a Pepsi bottle, you'd starve to death, but if you put Pepsi in a Coke bottle, you'd get rich quick," Smith recalled. His theory was that people were drinking Coke for its name, not its taste. "We were convinced people were drinking the trademark," Smith said, and that insight would provide the germ for an ingenious ploy.

But, despite these ideas, nothing was changing in Texas, and Smith continued to sweat it out under the gun from the Pepsi-Cola Company. He turned to the advertising mastermind Alan Pottasch for help, explaining that the nationwide Pepsi Generation theme wasn't working in the Lone Star State: "This image

stuff is great, but we're being outsold eight to one. We've got
to have a campaign that will move the needle." To Smith that
meant a campaign custom-made for his particular market.

Pottasch was opposed to local campaigns because such promotions were always product-oriented and would very likely
interfere with his carefully built emphasis on the user rather
than the beverage. Furthermore, if a one-market campaign
succeeded in one area, bottlers in other locations would get
wind of it and want it for their own territories even though
what works well in one place might not pay off in another. The
company would accrue additional costs for design and production, only to be left with an unwieldy, uncoordinated campaign.
Pottasch thought, too, that a local campaign would detract
from his coherent national one. "I was afraid it might create a
hole in the dike," he said, "and it did."

Smith, on the other hand, had nothing to lose—except his
job. He hired the in-house advertising agency of the Southland
Corporation's 7-11 convenience store chain, which accounted
for 50 percent of Pepsi's meager volume in Texas, to help him
come up with something. Bob Stanford, the creative director
there, did some field tests to determine how people felt about
Pepsi. Using a deceptively simple approach, he gave consumers a choice between two unmarked colas and asked them
which tasted better. Stanford filmed some of his unscientific
blind taste-tests and then gave Pottasch and Smith a screening.
Most people in the test chose Pepsi.

"We went back out in the field, this time with a hidden
camera, and—a little more like real research, but just barely—
we did a couple of hundred of these taste tests and then we
began to see the potential," Pottasch recalled. The tests gave

a slim but unmistakable fifty-two to forty-eight advantage to Pepsi. The beauty of comparative advertising is that a valid test that demonstrates a preference, however slim the margin, gives the advertiser the legal right to claim his product's superiority.

In May 1975 Pepsi ran with its claim in Dallas. The TV stations aired a somewhat crude commercial starring a succession of avowed Coke drinkers who were presented with two drinks, one labeled "Q" and one marked "M." They sipped from each, looked thoughtful for a moment, and when the announcer asked them to choose the better-tasting drink, they picked drink "M." The real identities of the drinks were then revealed, and behold, the taste-testers were astonished to see that their choice, potion "M," was Pepsi.

If the taste-testers were astonished, then the Coke faction was flabbergasted. Donald Keough was president of Coca-Cola USA when the "Pepsi Challenge" hit the Dallas airwaves. John Lupton, the world's largest bottler of Coke, called him with the news about Pepsi's Texas effrontery and, said Keough, "It was shocking."

The Coca-Cola Company responded quickly, though not very well. First they tried to disprove the claim and force Pepsi to remove its "misleading" advertising. But when they did their own test, they discovered something even more shocking: "It wasn't a false claim," said Keough. Coca-Cola had simply never tested its lead drink against any competitive product. "It wasn't allowed," he said. Keough and his marketing director, Ira ("Ike") Herbert, had suggested some tests a few years earlier but their idea had been met with "less than enthusiasm," as Herbert recalled. Coca-Cola's top management had made it clear that the secret formula, forever locked in a bank vault, was never to be tampered with. So even if Coca-Cola had performed its own comparative tests and discovered that Coke was not the preferred drink, it would never had changed the formula—or so Keough had to assume.

Pepsi's claim to taste superiority was intolerable to Keough, especially since this wasn't the only race that Coke seemed to be losing. In 1975 the A. C. Nielsen research firm's reports showed Pepsi edging out Coke in supermarkets nationwide; those sales represented about a third of Coke's total market. "When you are leader," Keough explained, "you want to lead all categories. Nielsen is the most visible. It's read by our investors, and the supermarkets were a growing market."

Fountain sales and vending/icebox sales made up the other two thirds of Coke's market. Now Atlanta executives had reason to worry about those areas too, since the company's contracts with such major fountain clients as McDonald's were based in large part on Coke's status as the number-one cola. If that claim fell—because of the Nielsen findings, because of the Pepsi Challenge—so might McDonald's pipeline to millions of Coke consumers. "You could write a scenario," said Keough, "that Pepsi's lead in the take-home could creep into fountain. Pepsi-Cola could use it as a selling story." At Coca-Cola's corporate headquarters many executives were jittery just imagining that scenario.

The Pepsi Challenge made them more nervous still. Those Dallas commercials were asking consumers to stop and reconsider. Why buy a trademark? Which drink tastes better? With even Coke enthusiasts on TV saying Pepsi tastes better, Coca-

Cola officials saw a threat to Coke's position. What was their response to the Pepsi Challenge?

"We tried to kid it off the air," Keough said.

Pepsi-Cola executives found the attempt pretty ludicrous. "The reaction from Coca-Cola astounded us," said Pottasch. "They came back with a commercial with this effeminate-sounding announcer saying something like 'They called our product "Q" and their product "M" and you know people like the letter "M" better.' "

Unbeknownst to Coca-Cola, Pepsi had filmed some tests in which Coke was labeled "L" and Pepsi "S." Even with the change of letters, Coke drinkers wound up picking Pepsi. "So the next day we hit them with that one," Pottasch said.

Coca-Cola countered with the message: "One sip is not enough." Coke contended that one brief taste might come out in favor of the sweeter drink but that with a whole glassful, you would appreciate the body and "zip" of Coke. Their next vengeful commercial "showed this Texas redneck Coke drinker saying that these outsiders were coming down to Texas and pulling their wily tricks, but that it wasn't going to work," recalled Pottasch. The Pepsi advertising director was rather startled that Coca-Cola would portray its consumers as Texas rednecks, but that aside, he was delighted that his ads were getting Coke's goat, and he also appreciated the recognition that Coca-Cola was giving its competition. "They played right into our hands . . . it was the first time they had ever mentioned Pepsi," Pottasch said.

"The Challenge took Pepsi's share from a six to a fourteen very quickly," said Smith, "and Coke went bananas." At Pepsi-

Cola headquarters in Purchase, New York, executives who hadn't even been shown the first commercials before they were aired were ecstatic. Smith had simply taken the bit and run with it, but luckily for him, the reaction was immediate and positive for Pepsi. The Challenge got an official okay, and pretty soon a hole broke in the dike, just as Pottasch had predicted. The Pepsi Challenge extended to Houston, where Coke enjoyed a 25 percentage point lead over Pepsi.

Coca-Cola couldn't muster a very strong defense on that front either. Roy Stout, the director of marketing research for Coca-Cola USA, recalled that when the Challenge began airing in Houston, Coca-Cola "had the bright idea of ending the Challenge with our "own taste tests" in that market. After all, Coke held a commanding share lead over "that other cola," and a taste test among what were obviously very loyal Coke drinkers would surely result in a major victory for Coke.

As it turned out, Stout's taste tests didn't reveal anything like a twenty-five-point lead. The figure was closer to four points, and Coca-Cola couldn't provide Pepsi-Cola with that kind of ammunition. So they took a rather circuitous route: Their new commercial showed a taste test that was not blind but where Pepsi and Coke were identified. The consumer picked Coke and the announcer played up the fact that Coke outsold Pepsi by six to one, and from those market share numbers it was implied that Coke must taste better than Pepsi.

Contrasting the attitudes and methods of the two cola companies, one executive with firsthand experience in both offices said, "Pepsi is much quicker to say what it thinks, much quicker to argue. It's hard to disagree at Coke. Pepsi is made up of fast-track MBAs, who take nothing for granted. Coke looks at Pepsi as ruthless, unpleasant, and with no loyalty. Coke values loyalty. Pepsi says let's get something done or be done. Donald Kendall, the PepsiCo chairman, once said he couldn't tell the difference between when the giant, Coca-Cola, was asleep or awake. At Pepsi, you don't have to like somebody to play with them." Before the gauntlet was thrown down, Coca-Cola would never have launched a comparative advertising campaign—that would have been considered mean, a breach of manners. Pepsi-Cola, on the other hand, was ready and waiting to step up its Challenge.

The new target in 1976 was Los Angeles. Pepsi and Coke had almost even market shares there, but polls revealed that residents perceived Coke as far outselling Pepsi. "We decided that wherever there was a perception that Coke was better, the Challenge would work," Pottasch said. "And it did."

By 1983 the Pepsi Challenge had spread around the country. It was airing in about 90 percent of the markets, and Pepsi-Cola had added other advertising techniques, such as in-store displays and packaging, which highlighted the new campaign. Only Coca-Cola's capital, Atlanta, was spared the insult of the Challenge, because Pepsi decided there was no sense in risking total retaliation by walking right into the lion's lair.

In the end, however, the Pepsi Challenge had an impact that was psychological rather than a matter of numbers. Both competitors now agree the Challenge never significantly hurt Coke's sales, at least in ways that can be measured. While the Challenge boosted Pepsi sales, they took away not from Coke's market share but from the shares of other soft-drink producers, as the beverage industry developed into a two-horse race. Records show that from 1975 until 1978 Coke's total market share actually increased slightly, from 24.2 percent of the market to 24.3 percent. During the same period Pepsi's share of the total market went from 17.4 percent to 17.6. (To interpret these figures, it should be remembered that 1 percent of the soft-drink industry during these years was the equivalent of $250,000,000 in retail sales.) Also, since the soft-drink industry was growing so rapidly, Coke's share, though it looked pretty stable, was actually growing more slowly than the industry as a whole. In 1975 Coca-Cola sold the equivalent of 1.1 billion cases of Coke, versus Pepsi's 775 million cases. By 1978 Coke was selling 1.3 billion cases and Pepsi 939 million. In 1979, although Coke's share of the overall soft-drink market dropped slightly from 24.3 percent to 23.9 percent, the brand's sales volume increased 2.2 percent. Pepsi's share also rose slightly from 17.6 percent to 17.9 percent in 1979, but its volume grew by 5.5 percent. In sum, the Pepsi Challenge did increase Pepsi's sales but not particularly at Coke's expense.

Even though Pepsi's challenge didn't directly affect Coca-Cola's pocketbook, it scored a victory which can't be measured by market share or volumes of sugar-water sold. "The pride of the company and bottlers was wounded," said Charles Millard, chairman of the New York bottling company. And wounded pride led to an obsession with Coke's image as number one.

This theme became the focus of Coca-Cola's next retaliation on TV. The company hired Bill Cosby, the popular comedian, to ridicule the Pepsi Challenge in a series of commercials known as the "Rat Pack," which referred to a pack of drinks that wished they were like Coke. "If you're number two or three or seven," Cosby mugged in the spots, "you know what you want to be when you grow up." And then he held up a can of Coke. "The number-one soft drink in the world. . . ."

Don Keough echoed that statement. "Coke is number one in the world and it should be number one in every way," he said.

"Fundamentally the rules changed. All of a sudden taste superiority became the point, such an important issue," explained Sergio Zyman, a Mexican-born dynamo who defected from Pepsi to Coca-Cola in 1979 and eventually became director of marketing for Coca-Cola USA. A thin, fit man with an abundance of carefully barbered curly hair, Zyman recalled the shift in focus at Coca-Cola during the onslaught of the Challenge, which lasted until 1983: "We were obsessed with the Pepsi Challenge and the Nielsen share—not sales."

The Pepsi Challenge indeed challenged the heart and soul of the Coca-Cola Company—its sacred cow, the secret formula, so secret that no more than three people at any time ever knew the proper mixture of its ingredients. "We had a formulation that had been in place since the dawn of our history, but consumers were changing and we shouldn't take it as a given that consumers' tastes hadn't changed," Keough said. "We should be certain that our product fit consumers' tastes and we shouldn't be embarrassed to explore."

So explore Coca-Cola did.

In 1979 Roy Stout, the director of marketing research, was given the first of several new colas to test. All he was told at the time was that it was a product the technical division said would beat Pepsi's taste. Stout's department conducted consumer taste tests and concluded that the new concoction, in fact, did *not* beat Pepsi. "It only tied Pepsi," Stout said. But at least the flavor chemists were getting closer; it was parity at least.

"The way it was left," Stout recalled, "was for the technical division to develop a taste that beat Pepsi, and then we'd decide what to do with it."

The Pepsi Challenge threatened Coca-Cola's heritage during a troubled decade, when the kingdom in Atlanta was fractured by civil wars and its leader was aging. The company's structure and practices were under attack. Perhaps Coca-Cola was feeling overly sensitive. Perhaps, as Millard said, "The company and some of the bottlers . . . overreacted to the Challenge." When Coca-Cola chose so drastic a course as exploring for a new formula, Pottasch felt "it had to be pride, because we weren't hurting their numbers. They overreacted and if they hadn't, history would have been different."

CHAPTER 5

DOING THINGS DIFFERENTLY

In 1979, 1,500 employees moved into Coca-Cola's new corporate headquarters in Atlanta, an imposing skyscraper of concrete, steel, and Sunset Beige granite rising twenty-six stories above North Avenue. The company's famous logo is carved into the granite outside the top four floors and emblazons the night sky with a red glow. Called the North Avenue Tower, the Coca-Cola building sits apart from Atlanta's skyline of banks, hotels, and office buildings like a patriarch receiving well wishers in the anteroom. To the citizens of Atlanta the grand new headquarters were a powerful reminder of Coca-Cola's power and prestige. Within the massive walls, however, on the top three floors—with their three-story atrium and skylight roof, their Georgian-styled offices, conference rooms, and dining rooms—executives yawned and stretched, waiting for someone to set things in motion. The company still lacked a new leader.

This instability at headquarters was kept well hidden because keeping up appearances was essential to Coca-Cola culture. Stay well dressed, look well-to-do, no matter what's happening. Not until November 1979, only three months before Austin was to retire as chairman and chief executive officer, did Coca-Cola finally reveal that he was staying on another year. At that point, news rippled through the executive ranks that Austin's successor would be selected from among the six vice-chairmen. "It was not a glorious time," recalled one candidate, Claus M. Halle, who was president of the Europe and Africa group. And Donald R. Keough, president of the Americas group, said the vice-chairmen were being shown around like prize bulls. Many thought that Keough with his high company profile, was destined for the job.

But out of the pool of executives rose an ambitious Cuban named Roberto C. Goizueta to challenge him. Goizueta, who joined the company in 1961, had not come up through the traditional marketing route as the other candidates had. A chemist by training, he had worked in the technical division, but Austin and Woodruff were quick to see he had more than scientific expertise to offer. Within two years after coming to Atlanta he was the company's youngest vice-president, earning $25,000 at age thirty-five, an excellent salary at that time. By 1972, when Keough arrived in Atlanta from the Houston–based foods division, Goizueta had made influential friends both inside and outside the company. His biggest and most important move came in 1974, when his office was moved to the same floor as that of Robert Woodruff. The Boss began inviting Goizueta to lunch, and that was the beginning of a unique friendship between two very different leaders.

The period of speculation dragged on and everyone at Coca-Cola wished that Austin would get around to making a decision. The salary charts from the company's proxy statements provided a clue, however. Only three of the executive vice-presidents were listed, meaning that they earned more than the other vice-chairmen, and Goizueta and Keough were the two in the lead. Goizueta earned $353,000 in salary and bonuses in 1978, and Keough, putting up a tough fight, followed closely at $330,000. By the next year, however, Goizueta's income had bolted ahead to $488,000, leaving Keough in the dust, relatively speaking, at $361,000.

The two rivals were in New York on February 14, 1980, to attend a birthday party for Austin being thrown by Edgar Bronfman, the chairman of Seagrams. After dinner at the Four Seasons, Goizueta and Keough had a few drinks in the St. Regis Hotel bar. They talked about who might become chairman, assuming it would be one of them, and they left the bar agreeing that whoever got the nod would make the other his right-hand man.

Finally, in April 1980, Austin called Goizueta into his office to announce that he was recommending him as the next chairman of the board. Austin then told Goizueta to hurry and see Woodruff before the old man took his after-lunch nap. Woodruff had suffered two strokes in the early seventies, and a weakened right side forced him to use a cane. Stubborn to the end, he had refused to be hospitalized after the strokes and now he refused to use a wheelchair. At ninety, however, the patriarch was finally ready to relinquish his power.

"How would you like to run my company?" Woodruff asked.

"It would be an honor and a challenge," Goizueta said. "I'd like to pick my own team."

"Fine."

"I'd like Don Keough to be my right-hand man."

"That'll be fine with me and fine with the board," Woodruff replied.

In fact, Woodruff and Goizueta were, by that time, very close. Woodruff regarded Goizueta almost as a son, and the younger man had enormous respect for the Boss. Even a few years after he had taken hold of the reins he still looked up to the man who had made Coca-Cola great. One day Woodruff said to him, "I'm very pleased now that you are boss." And Goizueta replied, "I'm not the boss."

"You're the chairman, aren't you?" persisted Woodruff.

"Yes."

"Then who's the boss?"

"The boss is the one who decides who's going to be chairman," said Goizueta.

In 1980 Goizueta was floored at the prospect of becoming the new chief and also at the way his appointment had occurred. There had been no formal vote of the board. Woodruff said they'd approve the selection, and they did. On May 30, 1980, the board named Goizueta president, with the understanding that he would assume the duties of the chairman in March 1981. Don Keough was named senior executive vice-president, and it was clear that he would succeed Goizueta as president and chief operating officer in March. All operations would report to Goizueta through Keough, who emerged as "the buffer" for the quick-tempered Goizueta. Keough was the amicable, patient manager to Goizueta's perfectionism. Their tandem performance could be likened to a bad cop–good cop method of operation. The two complemented each other— Goizueta, the aloof, tenacious strategist, and Keough, the gregarious and smooth persuader.

Many Coca-Cola officials, not to mention the ladies and gentlemen of Atlanta's old-line families, were stunned at the appointment of a Cuban to the top spot in a southern old-boy regime. But Goizueta was not so unlikely a candidate. He was an aristocrat in the tradition of the Southern upper class, and like Woodruff, he was a third-generation aristocrat who had made it on his own.

Forced to flee Cuba in 1961 after Castro's rise to power, Goizueta left behind millions of dollars in real estate, sugar and lumber holdings, though not the manners and self-confidence of the privileged. He brought to Atlanta a flair for eloquence and a taste for immaculate, well-tailored clothes.

Goizueta's intelligence is as impressive as his appearance. He has an astounding memory, which he attributes to his primary and secondary education under the Jesuits at the Colegio de Belen in Havana, where he was forced to memorize biblical and academic passages. After high school Goizueta decided he wanted a degree in chemical engineering from Yale University, but to qualify, he had to spend a year at Cheshire Academy in Connecticut working mostly on his English. He memorized his way through the year's lessons and graduated as valedictorian. At Yale, Goizueta recalled, "I had to memorize; it was the only way I could pass. I had to read and reread and I had to concentrate."

In his personal life and in his business methods, Goizueta endorses a saying by Friedrich Nietzsche: "God is in the details." Nothing brings a quicker reproach from the chairman's office than a factual error, no matter how trivial. The guilty party receives a memo with Goizueta's message scrawled across the top: "Facts are Facts." The press, too, has been blasted by Goizueta on more than one occasion. Any criticism of himself or the company that he feels is unfounded—not based on facts —sets him off, and he sends meticulous corrections to reporters while his public-relations staff shudders. Even a technical slip, such as the use of "fructose" to mean "high-fructose corn syrup," elicits a long pedantic letter to the reporter and the editor.

Goizueta would need all his mental powers to deal with the troubled company he had inherited. The job was no sinecure; rather, it was as if you had worked for years to finally become boss, only to discover that what you'd won was the right to preside over a façade.

Although Goizueta had suspicions about the company's failings, the full extent of the problems surfaced only during his "Spanish Inquisition." This ordeal, so called because of Goizueta's hard questioning, was a two-week-long meeting held in October 1980. For the first time in the company's history, the heads of divisions and operations from around the world were told to present a three-year plan for their units.

"We found that the actions taken by these leaders were guided more by what the competition was doing than as a result of any analysis of what *we* should be doing," said Goizueta. "One unit would go after sales and another after market share, based on what he believed was best for the company. But there was no overall strategy by which any were making these decisions." Throughout the 155 countries in which Coke is distributed, officials held entirely different views of the company and very different ideas about how to operate.

Goizueta and Keough and John Collings, the chief financial officer, quickly learned that a crucial part of their job was to reverse earlier business decisions and institute the standard business practices, which had been blithely ignored in the seventies. "We had lost sight of return on capital," Goizueta discovered. Information about the results of such inefficiency snowballed as the meeting progressed. Collings detected the company's losses in the fountain business. The Wine Spectrum loomed as a fiasco, as did Aqua-Chem, both of which represented the company's unfortunate attempts at diversification.

"Now," proclaimed Goizueta, "don't even come to us with a project that doesn't yield more money than the cost of money; you'll get no hearing, much less a 'no.'"

All the evidence the new management team could gather seemed to indicate that significant growth in soft-drink volume was no longer in the cards. The annual growth rate of the company's worldwide soft-drink volume had dropped from the 10 percent of earlier years to 3.3 percent by 1980. Many beverage experts were saying that as America grew older, fewer soft drinks would be consumed. Demographers were clear on this point: by 1990 the under-twenty age group would decline from 38 percent of the U.S. population to 29 percent, and by the turn of the century, 50 percent of the population would be at least fifty years old. Since the under-thirty crowd accounts for 44 percent of all soft drinks consumed, *Business Week*'s May 1977 cover story on the graying of America made many Coca-Cola executives even less optimistic about the future of soft drinks.

(We know now that those predictions did not work out. In 1975 Americans consumed 33 billion gallons of beverages. By 1985 the figure had risen to 37 billion. More significant, soft drinks' share went from 16 percent in 1975 to 25 percent in 1985.)

"If in 1981 somebody had said that soft-drink volume in the United Sttaes in 1985 would have grown 8 percent, we would have said he was crazy," Goizueta remarked. "We missed our forecasts on how vibrant the soft-drink industry would be." While this misreading would not really affect the sales of Coke, it would change the structure of the company and its way of thinking. "We felt we had to get into industries with inherent growth potential, where the forces would work in our favor," said Goizueta.

By the end of the Spanish Inquisition, then, the triumvirate knew without doubt that the Coca-Cola Company was in need of a major overhaul and a rejuvenation of purpose. For Coca-Cola to enter the modern age of commerce and fight back the Pepsi Challenge, many changes, including a cultural one, would have to occur within the company.

Keough and Collings worked together over the next few months, boiling down their conclusions from the meeting into a rough-draft report to Goizueta, who then wrote his vision of the company in the 1980s. In March 1981, he called a worldwide manager's conference for fifty-one of this international company's "movers and shakers," who had been moving in uncoordinated directions and who needed shaking up if, as Keough said, "we were to pick up the drumbeat."

"If we could have seen a 10 percent real growth in earnings," said Goizueta, "or a return on equity of 20 percent, we wouldn't have called the meeting. But we needed to do things differently or do different things, and we did both."

Palm Springs, California, is a desert playground where opulence abounds and the sun shines year round. But the Coca-Cola executives who met at Marriott's Rancho Las Palmas Resort didn't get to play any golf or tennis. At the five-day meeting, starting March 28, sessions began at eighty-thirty in the morning and ran until dinner. Business continued right through that meal and into the night, when Keough would hold court in the hotel's bar.

Most new management teams hold such meetings of their top staff to tell the chosen few that a new day has dawned and that they are part of a historic beginning. But at Palm Springs, Goizueta set an entirely different tone right from the start. The company was going to change, he announced, and its managers had better change with it. "Those who don't adapt will be left behind or out—no matter what level they are," he said.

Before launching his attack on the very heart and soul of the Coca-Cola Company, Goizueta launched into a lesson in semantics. He wanted to let his team know that there was a big difference, in his view, between planning and strategy: "I happen not to like the term 'strategic planning,' because it can lead to misinterpretations. To my mind, corporate strategy deals with what we want to be as a company, and planning, and specifically long-range planning, deals with how we become what we want to be. This may seem like an exercise in semantic hairsplitting, but it is in fact critical to our collective understanding of our ground rules or operating philosophy for the future."

Goizueta went on to debunk the long-cherished theory that Coca-Cola's success came from its marketing expertise; he pointed to Procter & Gamble as real marketing stars. He also attacked the company's other sacred cows: a distribution system reputed to be the best in the world, and the idea that Coca-Cola could do whatever it wanted to without taking risks. He mocked the company's so-called broad technical strengths, saying that processing orange juice concentrate didn't make one an expert in agriculture.

Goizueta then called for a radical change in what Coca-Cola prided itself on most—its culture. Coca-Cola executives had come to believe that what they looked like was more important than what they contributed, that if they put on a pinstripe suit and stayed clean-shaven, they could do no wrong. According to Goizueta, Coca-Cola had been content to protect the status quo, cautious to question, and late to act. All of that had to change if the company was to thrive. "The only company that continues to enjoy success is the company that keeps struggling to achieve it," he said. "A company starts to worry about holding on to success when it's decided it has more to lose than it has to gain, and at that point, it gets timid and overly concerned with appearances."

As Goizueta neared the end of his speech, he encouraged the executives to debate any issue they wished. "Just to give you an example that there are no sacred cows . . . , let me assure you at the outset that such things as the reformulation of any or all of our products will not stand in the way of giving any of our competitors a real or a perceived product advantage. The days are gone in which an inflexible adherence to a sacred cow will ever give renewed impetus and breathe life into a competitor like it happened when we chose to stick only with the six-and-a-half-ounce bottle for a number of years when our main competitor was going to a larger size."

The far-reaching implications of this last remark were not lost on some of the executives. Doug Ivester, a comptroller at Coca-Cola, recalled that as Goizueta was making those comments, he thought, "They're going to change the formula."

During the next four days, the managers grappled with issues ranging from human resources and energy costs to the bottling franchises and financial reporting. For the first time, the top executives of Coca-Cola's U.S. and international operations were told that profits and shareholders were the driving forces behind the company—a simple enough notion, all right, but one that had not heretofore guided the Coca-Cola Company.

To set managers straight about the business environment of the eighties, Goizueta had invited to the conference a business consultant named Michael Kami. The head planner for IBM until 1968, Kami now lived on a yacht at Lighthouse Point, Florida, enjoying a contemplative life and working about three months a year.

Before going to Palm Springs, Kami had studied the Coca-Cola Company. "I discovered what I thought," he said. "Coca-Cola was nice—successful and conservative—but other than the Coke name, it was dull."

Kami at first was skeptical about how much the company could change, but when he met and talked with Goizueta, he said, he had a feeling that something was going to happen. No wonder. The two are kindred souls, philosophers in a corporate world, who speak each other's language.

Kami's advice was that "management must make decisions

three times faster than in the past, and in order to do that, companies must have flexible organizations—you can't have paralysis through analysis. Develop a more horizontal organization, have better communications, put in the ultimate in automation and increase productivity."

Kami also told his audience that they could no longer be content with producing one product but would have to enter the "fierce competition in a non-homogeneous market."

Kami left the executives with a saying that was to become a sort of buzz question: "How many times have you been turned down?" In other words, if you want to be an entrepreneur within a large corporation, you must keep pushing your ideas. You haven't asked often enough if you haven't been turned down.

Goizueta and his speakers churned up the executives by undermining their complacency, challenging their vision of the Coca-Cola Company, and forcing them to take stock of the modern world. That was precisely the atmosphere Goizueta wanted for presenting his "Strategy Statement." His carefully conceived, simple statement was to provide a standard by which the company could measure itself in the following years. It had been approved in advance by the board of directors, and Goizueta warned the managers not to regard what he would say as generalities—"and don't take it lightly."

He began, "The unique position of excellence that the product Coca-Cola has attained in the world will be protected and enhanced as a primary objective. . . . I perceive us by the 1990s continuing to be, or becoming, the dominant force in the soft-drink industry in each of the countries in which it is economically feasible for us to be so. . . . It is most likely that we will be in industries which we are not in today. We will not, however, stray far from our major strengths: an impeccable and positive image with the consumer; a unique franchise system second to none; and the intimate knowledge of, and contacts with, local business conditions around the world."

Goizueta went on to emphasize the company's commitment to its shareholders. "Increasing annual earnings per share and effecting increased return on equity are still the name of the game—but," he added, "not to the extent that our longer-term viability is threatened."

Goizueta then turned to the company's "life-style," and to the qualities that his managers would have to have in order to see his vision realized. He stressed courage, commitment, integrity, and fairness, but the real emphasis seemed to be on taking initiatives rather than simply reacting: "It is my desire that we encourage intelligent individual risk-taking." He also hoped the company would have "the sensitivity to anticipate and adapt to change—change in consumer life-styles, change in consumer tastes, and change in consumer needs."

Most of Goizueta's speech was made public in a printed pamphlet. Many senior executives would keep it in plain view on their desks at all times, but certain outsiders found Goizueta's vision so simple that they didn't take it seriously. Only when the company began acting on the speech did they appreciate Goizueta's commitment to change.

At the Palm Springs meeting, Goizueta did discuss some specifics of his program, which were not made public. For instance, Coca-Cola had hired Arthur D. Little, a consulting firm, to help identify companies that Coca-Cola should consider buying. Goizueta told the managers that he would not "preclude the company's involvement in the communications industry or personal-care products," and in fact, investigations in those areas were already under way. Industrial businesses, however, were not the company's forte, and a decision had been made to sell Aqua-Chem. Above all, the top managers of Coca-Cola saw possibilities in the entertainment industry, and Ira Herbert, soon to be the new corporate marketing director, had already talked with a key executive at Columbia Pictures Industries, Incorporated.

There was another subtler but perhaps more critical change in the way Goizueta would do things, but he himself was unaware of it. His appointment as boss of Coca-Cola had put a first-generation immigrant in charge of a quintessentially American company. And he was not the only relative newcomer to the United States among Coca-Cola's senior executives. The company's melting pot included, among others, Sergio Zyman, a first-generation Mexican who was vice-president in charge of bottling operations; and Brian Dyson, the Argentinian president of Coca Cola USA who had come to the United States only in 1978. After John Collings's death in 1981, Egyptianborn Sam Ayoub was named chief financial officer, prompting Keough to joke that he was the token American. Certainly no one official proffered views that were in any way out of step with American ways of doing things, but the fact that many foreigners had high positions may have had a cumulative effect. How could anyone who had been in a country for only five or ten years understand fully the depth of its symbols and realize completely the meaning of its traditions? Perhaps, then, Goizueta and his team underestimated the significance of Coca-Cola to the American people and saw only indistinctly that Coke is as American as Babe Ruth and baseball, as mom and apple pie. And that there are some things you just don't change.

CHAPTER 6

COKE GOES HOLLYWOOD

The first steps in the mating dance between the Coca-Cola Company and Columbia Pictures took place on a cold, rainy night in November 1981, behind the iron gates of the "21" Club in New York. To accommodate Donald Keough, a valued customer, the restaurant had cleared a second-floor dining room, leaving fifteen tables unoccupied at dinner time, so that the top executives of the two companies could talk in privacy. When Herbert Allen, chairman of Columbia, first was invited to the meeting, he thought that Coca-Cola wanted to talk about investing in Columbia movies. But the arrangement at the "21" Club, he realized, boded something more dramatic. He said, "That's when I thought it might be serious. It was like clearing Grand Central Station when you wanted to look over the time schedule."

In fact, under Goizueta's tutelage, the new Coca-Cola Company was enthusiastically moving ahead with its commitment to change and diversification. Its consulting firm, Arthur D. Little, had recommended that Coca-Cola get into the entertainment business, specifically into a motion-picture studio with an extensive film library. By a process of elimination, Columbia had been targeted. MCA was too big and Lew Wasserman, one of its principal owners, would probably not want to sell. Warner Bros. was too diversified, and Paramount was buried deep in the corporate bowels of Gulf & Western. Columbia, on the other hand, was relatively small, about a tenth the size of Coca-Cola, and it was operating profitably under a new management. The real drawing card, though, was Columbia's library of about eighteen hundred films. Unlike some motion picture companies, Columbia always retained all rights to its films, never selling them outright. Coca-Cola coveted that asset.

Because a Columbia board member and a Coca-Cola executive were good friends, Coca-Cola was able to get firsthand information about how business was going at the film company. Karl Eller, who had built the Combined Communications Corporation empire later purchased by the Gannett Company, had joined Columbia in 1979. He thought highly of its management team and said as much to Ike Herbert, Coca-Cola's director of corporate marketing. Eller suggested a meeting between the Coca-Cola executives and Columbia's Herbert Allen and Francis Vincent, its president. Despite Coca-Cola's self-confidence, Columbia was not particularly eager to get involved. It had already successfully fought off a takeover attempt by an investor, Kirk Kerkorian, in 1979. And though the company had been on the verge of bankruptcy in the early seventies, it was now in excellent shape, enjoying a string of box-office hits including *Close Encounters of the Third Kind* and *Kramer Versus*

Kramer. Columbia was also in the process of buying the Outlet Company with its seven TV and radio stations for $166.5 million.

Herb Allen, the Chairman of Columbia, came from a family of investment bankers: His father and uncle were the founding partners of the Wall Street investment firm Allen & Company. In 1973, with cash to invest and feeling a little "bored," Allen got involved in Columbia by accident." His friend Ray Stark, the producer of *Funny Girl*, urged him to come to Columbia and save the studio. After examining the situation, Allen made a $2.5 million investment—one that would yield $40 million nine years later.

In the "21" Club dining room that November night Allen and "Fay" Vincent met with Keough, Herbert, and Eller. Goizueta didn't make an appearance, the strategy being that if the meeting went poorly, the Coca-Cola representatives could later back out of negotiations by telling Columbia that the chairman had changed his mind.

Throughout most of the dinner the executives made small talk, gingerly trying to get acquainted. Vincent sat next to Keough. "I was stunned that an Iowan Irish Catholic was president of that southern institution Coca-Cola," Vincent recalled. "My stereotype of Coca-Cola was out of the Jimmy Carter and Bert Lance mold."

It was getting around time for dessert when Keough finally began his sales pitch. He told Allen and Vincent that Coca-Cola had looked at the acquisition of various new business ventures and had narrowed the categories to two—ethical drugs and entertainment—but had finally decided that the latter would be a better fit. (The drug business had been rejected because of the unpredictability of the time between a research-and-development investment and the production of a marketable drug.) Keough stressed Coca-Cola's interest in home entertainment and pointed to Columbia's ample film library, from which video cassettes would pour, as well as the company's other desirable attributes. Any merger of the companies would have to be entirely friendly, he said, as it was not Coca-Cola's nature to attempt hostile corporate takeovers.

Though Allen might have been surprised at Coca-Cola's impending offer, he knew all too well how to play the game of mergers and acquisitions. Without directly addressing the issue, he coolly made it clear to Keough at this early stage that, if any merger was to take place, he would insist on a premium price. "It will knock your eyes out," he joked.

Dinner was adjourned with the agreement that another meeting would be held as soon as possible. Allen and Vincent walked out of the "21" Club together into the chilly night. Vincent was as close to euphoria as a characteristically reserved northeasterner could be. His years of patient lawyering, his stamina in spite of a crippling back injury, his endurance and grace in the face of Hollywood backbiting and, above all, his honorable conduct were about to pay off handsomely. He was about to become a squeaky clean millionaire and the Coca-Cola Company was about to validate his entire business career.

"Great company," Vincent said to Allen.

For Allen, already a millionaire, the deal was just that—a deal, and no more.

"I bet we make a deal," said Vincent.

"I don't, because wait until they see the price I'm going to ask," Allen answered.

Executives from both companies next met at Columbia's Fifth Avenue offices in December, and this time Chairman Goizueta was in attendance, as was Sam Ayoub, Coke's new chief financial officer.

The picture Herb Allen painted of his company was almost as rosy as the Coca-Cola logo. First, Columbia got 25 percent of its movies' production costs from outside investors, thereby reducing the risk of losses from box-office bombs. Feature films generated most of Columbia's profits, and the television division, particularly the TV syndication arm, was also a gold mine. Columbia didn't have to risk much up front on its TV shows—hits or misses—because the networks bore most of the production costs. And once a show was on the air for three or four years, syndication rights could be sold to stations across the country. Such shows as *Barney Miller* brought in huge chunks of cash for syndication rights alone: in 1981, the funny policemen of the Greenwich Village precinct earned Columbia $42 million. And the following year *Charlie's Angels* pulled in another $23 million. Allen told the group of enticing future prospects of pay-per-view programming on cable television and videocassette sales and rentals, fires to be stoked by Columbia's future productions as well as its film library.

Allen also wanted Goizueta to know that he and Vincent were merely the moneymen at Columbia—they took care of the budgets and financing—but had absolutely no say in the editorial content of the pictures. "I have never even read a script," said the chairman.

Allen was also shrewd enough to bring up some potential problems at Columbia, before his would-be partners did, and to turn those too into bargaining ploys. He recited a litany of negatives such a pristine company as Coca-Cola should weigh before diving into the glamorous and dangerous waters of Hollywood.

"This tiny little company is always going to be in the press," Allen told the Coca-Cola executives. "From the amount of coverage we get, you would think we were AT&T. And if someone in New York sneezes, somebody in California says 'Bless you.'"

Goizueta reported that they had already reviewed the press infatuation with Hollywood and had decided Coca-Cola could live with it.

Allen then said he knew that Coca-Cola's board was weighted with elderly men who might object when Columbia produced sexy movies.

Goizueta replied that Coca-Cola would have trouble with X-rated movies, but that otherwise there wouldn't be a problem.

Allen then mentioned the incredibly high salaries of Hollywood movie executives, who made more money than the men they worked for in New York. Frank Price, the studio chief, earned twice Vincent's salary and bonus, even though Vincent had the power to fire him.

Goizueta said he could live with that too, as long as this high-priced talent produced. "If they don't, then it might bother me."

Allen didn't hesitate to bring up the biggest skeleton in Columbia's closet—the Begelman scandal. Like practically everyone else in Hollywood, Allen knew that a book about the affair would be published during the next year, in 1982. It would be highly critical of Columbia in general and Allen in particular.

David Begelman had been caught embezzling some $70,000,

and the ensuing fight between Allen and Alan Hirschfield, then
president of Columbia, had been very nasty and very public.
Even though the story was five years old, the juicy details were
sure to turn up on best-seller lists.

Allen told Coca-Cola then what he still says today: that
Begelman, who was earning hundreds of thousands of dollars
and held stock options worth a million or more, had forged
three checks, whose total was a pittance in comparison with his
income; that doctors and the courts had determined that he was
suffering from emotional problems; that the Columbia board
took away his hefty stock options; that he was removed as a
director and stripped of his title. Begelman had been suspended,
but Hirschfield wanted him fired. Allen disagreed violently because he thought Begelman should have a second chance: "He
was sick—which the doctors and the courts concurred with—
so we penalized him and then tried to deal with him as a
human. We tried to rehabilitate him, but that was the wrong
decision, given the PR of the day, post Watergate." This argument constituted Allen's defense against both Hirschfield and
the account that eventually appeared in the book *Indecent
Exposure*.

Both Goizueta and Keough accepted Allen's version. When
the manuscript of *Indecent Exposure* was in galley proofs, Allen
procured a copy and sent it to Goizueta, who says he read only
a little before he quit in disgust at the author's assertions.
Keough has a copy of the book, but he says he hasn't read it
either.

When Allen had finished briefing Goizueta and the other
Coca-Cola executives, he told them that if Coca-Cola wanted to
buy Columbia, the price would seem "exorbitant." "We feel

comfortable [independent] and think we are the best in the business," he said matter-of-factly. "We have to have a price we can't turn down."

At that point no specific price was named, both sides presenting a bargainer's front until financial teams could "run the numbers" to ascertain Columbia's assets and value.

With all his business savvy and foresight, Allen remained pessimistic about this deal. "I think they are going to say forget it," he told Vincent. Vincent disagreed and added that there was another advantage to the sale: the acquisition by Coca-Cola would be viewed by the public as a vindication of Allen. The financial community would credit Allen with cleaning up Columbia so well after the Begelman scandal that a company of Coca-Cola's stature would want it.

"It's time to end this chapter," Vincent said. "We should finish it up. We cleaned it up and now it will be their company."

The people of the Coca-Cola Company were hardly the sharp bargainers that the practiced deal-makers at Columbia were. According to a later assessment by Goizueta, Coca-Cola's negotiating skills, such as they were, had grown out of the company's dealings with its own bottlers. Since the health and wealth of the bottlers was bound up with that of Coca-Cola, arrangements between the two were usually friendly and based on mutual benefit. These negotiations didn't require flushing out vulnerabilities and capitalizing on them, nor much bluffing either.

Columbia's executives, in contrast, were veteran players trained in Hollywood, where nothing can happen without a multitude of deals, often elaborate ones. The bidding for and buying of scripts and the contractual agreements between authors, actors, studios, directors, producers, and so on constitute so much of Hollywood existence that on studio lots there are more lawyers, agents, and wheeler-dealers than there are full-time actors. The Coca-Cola Company, which was thirsting for a piece of the entertainment business, was about to experience a rite of passage into a world beyond its own domain.

On Sunday, January 17, 1982, several hectic weeks after the New York meeting, the Columbia team met with the Coca-Cola team on the twenty-sixth floor of Coca-Cola's headquarters in Atlanta. It was a make-or-break day for both companies. There had been enough talk and enough number crunching. It was time to shake hands or walk away.

Allen's role was to set the price. Columbia's stock had been trading recently in the $40-per-share range—about ten times what he had paid for his shares in 1973. Now he based his asking price on what he thought Columbia's stock might be worth in two or three years. In short, he wanted a hefty, unqualified premium. Allen hadn't even told his associates what he was going to ask, keeping his teammates in the dark until the last possible moment to avoid the kind of second-guessing that can kill a deal. The chairman opened the negotiations at a staggering $85 per share, more than twice the stock's current value. "At least none of my people laughed," he later remarked.

Goizueta, Keough, and Ayoub had come to the meeting with a "choking price" in mind, but Allen's figure blew the lid off their highest limit. "That's so far off it isn't funny," exclaimed Goizueta. He had figured that Coca-Cola would have to pay a sort of entry fee because they were getting into a new business and couldn't estimate Columbia's worth quite as precisely as they could the value of another soft-drink business. They knew they wanted Columbia and their thinking was like that of a person buying a dream house who is willing to pay a premium price rather than bargain and lose to another bidder. But the $85 per share being asked put the price tag for Columbia at nearly $1 billion.

The meeting adjourned and the two groups went into separate rooms to confer. Allen gazed out the window and saw in the distance Stone Mountain, a curious outcropping of granite some twenty miles east of Atlanta.

"That's some mountain," he said. "Wonder how far it is from here?"

"About as far away as we are from getting eighty-five dollars," said one of his associates.

Back in the negotiating room together, financial officer Ayoub said that $85 wouldn't work. He then opened his briefcase and pulled out a manila envelope. Columbia's president Vincent could see that there were other envelopes and he figured that they represented different offers. So before Ayoub could speak, Vincent said, "Forget that one, Sam, and go to the next envelope." Coca-Cola was learning fast—never let the other guy see into your briefcase.

Coca-Cola's counter offer was $68. Columbia said $82.

Coca-Cola bid $72. Columbia asked $75.

And got it.

"We were stunned," Vincent recalled, and the Columbia executives would not be alone in their reaction.

On Tuesday, January 19, 1982, Coca-Cola announced that it would pay approximately $750 million in cash and stocks for Columbia Pictures. The immediate torrent of publicity was so enormous that Roberto Goizueta was shocked. It was a vivid lesson that whatever Coca-Cola did attracted an inordinate amount of attention in the nation's press.

Not only was there a lot of publicity, but nearly all of it was sharply critical of the deal. Wall Street's securities analysts thought the acquisition unwise, and Coca-Cola's stock price lost around 10 percent of its value in the first few days following the announcement. Goizueta got angry. Hadn't he already let the world know that Coca-Cola was casting around for new industries, even pinpointing entertainment as a likely target? Why were they so shocked—and so negative? He was especially annoyed at the beverage industry analysts, who suddenly professed to be experts in the entertainment business and came down hard on Coca-Cola's acquisition.

There were those who thought the deal made sense, but even they thought Coca-Cola had been robbed. "They took a lot of heat for paying that high a price," Allen commented. Today, Goizueta admits that Coca-Cola probably paid 10 percent to 15 percent too much, but he says that by doing so they made sure that no other competing offers landed on the table.

"We'd heard that Time Inc. wanted Columbia," Goizueta says.

As it turned out, not only did Coca-Cola get there first, but they added to their ranks the superb negotiating team that now, on Coke's behalf, would run circles around Time Inc.

In November 1982, HBO (Home Box Office), the pay-television service owned by Time Inc., proudly announced a joint-venture deal with Columbia and CBS. Among those who knew the details, however, the joke was that Coke had paid $750 million for Columbia, and Time paid about the same to rent Columbia for three years.

For some months prior to November, Columbia had been trying to work out a licensing and coproduction deal with either HBO or Showtime, a similar competitive service. Columbia wanted a pay-cable movie channel to help finance its movies in exchange for the exclusive rights to show them.

Vincent approached Time first and offered to buy a minority interest in HBO. When he was turned down he went to Showtime. Columbia, in a joint proposal with ABC and 20th Century-Fox, began negotiating to buy 25 percent to 33 percent of Showtime and to form a new production studio. The deal looked promising to everyone concerned and they were on the verge of firming it up when—without discussing it with ABC and 20th Century-Fox—Vincent decided to give Time one more stab at the action. He called Richard Munro, the chief executive officer of Time. "I told him we were going to do a deal with Showtime and that I wasn't trying to pressure him, but I didn't want him to come back six months later and say that he didn't realize we were serious."

In effect, this overture would leave ABC and Fox standing at the altar.

Munro, of course, was also shocked at the impending deal and "all hell broke loose," said Vincent. "Suddenly HBO was asking us what it would take to stop us from doing the Showtime deal. We backed ourselves into the greatest position in life. HBO and CBS were trying to get enough on my plate so I wouldn't do Showtime, and our guys were better negotiators. We put the ball over the fence. It was a huge transaction. There was a lot of criticism but it didn't take long before people realized it was a major coup."

HBO agreed to finance 25 percent of the production cost of every Columbia movie, as a guarantee against the license fee, with no ceiling on the production cost.

"If we made a $10 million picture, they paid $2.5 million," Vincent explained. "But it was tied to rentals [the studio's revenues from box office receipts], so if the movie did $12 million in rentals, they paid us $4 million as a license fee, but if the movie didn't make a dime, they still paid us $2.5 million. On top of that," said Vincent, "they agreed to finance 25 percent of the movie cost as an equity partner. So, they ended up financing fifty to sixty percent of our production costs. Then CBS paid us $2 million per picture for the TV rights."

At the same time that Columbia made its deal with HBO, the three entertainment companies (Columbia, CBS, and Time) also formed a joint-venture motion-picture studio called Tri-Star Pictures. HBO and CBS agreed to basically the same terms for financing and licensing Tri-Star's films as it had with Columbia. The only difference was that Columbia skimmed off an additional fee of 12.5 percent of the rentals in return for distributing Tri-Star's movies.

"We had a pipeline to Time Inc.'s treasury," said Vincent.

Indeed. With HBO's license fee pegged to how well a Tri-Star or a Columbia movie did at the box office, the Time unit sometimes paid more to show the movie than it had cost to produce it. For example, in 1985, HBO paid a license fee of $36 million for *Ghostbusters*, which cost $35 million to produce.

"That broke the bank," Vincent remarked, and by early 1985 Time asked for relief. When HBO had made the deal in 1982, it was the star of cable TV. HBO was growing by leaps and bounds—from a mere 365 subscribers in 1972 to 11 million ten years later—and many felt it would add at least 2 million subscribers annually. It didn't turn out that way, and the cable TV industry over the next couple of years was plagued by shakeouts, shutdowns, and general malaise. At the end of 1984, HBO had only 14.5 million subscribers and was no longer forecasting a growth rate like that of its first decade. By the end of 1985, HBO could count 14.6 million subscribers. As the growth of its pay-television service declined, HBO was still strapped with sky-high programming costs, and Time suffered an uncomfortable squeeze on its profits.

Columbia finally agreed to renegotiate with Time to reduce the onerous clauses. They placed a ceiling on the production costs and license fees and extended the deal to 1992.

"We murdered them the first time because we made them do it quickly, but Coca-Cola is not in business to murder its partners," Vincent acknowledged.

"My position was 'Why should we sacrifice for their poor forecasts?'" Goizueta said of the 1985 deal renegotiation. But the contract put the two partners on better terms, and at last Goizueta became reconciled to the compromise, commenting, "No point in hating each other when you have to live with each other."

Coca-Cola's acquisition of Columbia proved to be a triumph for the company's reputation and for its pocketbook.* It was a

---

* By 1985, Coca-Cola's entertainment division included Embassy Communications and Tandem Productions, which were acquired for approximately $445 million in cash and stock.

personal coup for Goizueta, firing up his confidence and pride, which were scarcely diminutive to begin with. Within six months after the purchase the press was beginning to change its tune. On the one-year anniversary of the announcement the headline of the *Wall Street Journal's* "Heard on the Street" column ran: "Coca-Cola's Acquisition of Columbia Pictures in Hindsight Looks Like a Good Move to Analysts." Skeptical Wall Street and stock analysts were taking another look at Coca-Cola and replacing their derisive criticism with praise.

The numbers soon showed just how wrong those analysts and reporters had been, and Goizueta relished telling them so. Coca-Cola had predicted in 1982 that by 1985 Columbia would contribute $90 million to the company's operating income, but Columbia achieved that figure by 1983. By 1985 the motion-picture company was contributing 14 percent of Coca-Cola's operating income, edging out the Foods Division as the number-two contributor, though still lagging far behind the soft-drink division. And in terms of profits, the entertainment division was the largest in the country, if not in the world, surpassing Gulf and Western, Warner, and MCA.

Along with its handsome profits from Columbia, Coca-Cola added new blood to its staff—3,800 new employees and two brilliant leaders who would become indispensable advisors to Goizueta and Keough.

At the outset, however, Allen and Vincent didn't envision a long, happy union with the owner company. "We all thought that after one year, we'd leave and go do it again," Vincent said. He also anticipated that most of Columbia's top management would be replaced, as happens in most mergers. "I didn't think I was relevant," said the Columbia president.

In fact, Allen and Vincent proved to be an excellent fit at Coca-Cola. More like Coca-Cola executives than Hollywood moguls, they are members of the northeastern establishment, politically moderate, financially conservative, and traditional. Goizueta asked Allen onto the board in 1982, but Allen, who is not a joiner of clubs or committees, was reluctant. "I was acting out of ignorance," he later acknowledged. "Then Fay convinced me that Columbia needed a hook into the parent company," said Allen and he finally accepted. He is still on the board four years later, largely because of his close relationship with Goizueta. "Only friendship has kept Allen on the board," said Vincent. "There is no other force on earth that could have kept him there." Just as Goizueta and Allen have paired off, so have Vincent and Keough. The president of Columbia, who was named head of Coca-Cola's entertainment section in 1983, talks with Keough several times a week. "If I hadn't liked Don, I would have been doing something else," confessed Vincent, "and if Allen hadn't liked Roberto, he would be too."

Today Allen is often one of the first directors Goizueta calls for advice, and he has found life at Coca-Cola more exciting than he anticipated. What did he expect back in 1982? "A big, dry, dull typical American corporation, unwilling to take risks," he said.

CHAPTER 7

"JUST FOR THE TASTE OF IT"

In 1920, the United States Supreme Court, in one of the few trademark cases the high court had ever reviewed, ruled in favor of the Coca-Cola Company, which had accused such imitators as the Koke Company of America of violating its trademarks, "Coke" and "Coca-Cola." Justice Oliver Wendell Holmes, writing the opinion for the court, held that the trademarks "Coke" and "Coca-Cola" denoted a single beverage. "The name now characterizes a beverage to be had at almost any soda fountain. It means a single thing coming from a single source and well known to the community."

The phrase "a single thing coming from a single source" became a benchmark in trademark law, and at the Coca-Cola Company it became a pledge of allegiance, an oath repeated over and over again wherever anyone dared bring up the idea of extending the trademark to another product.

In 1962, the innovative Royal Crown Cola Company introduced the first nationally distributed diet cola. Diet-Rite became a hit in a nation becoming increasingly worried about
weight control.

The Coca-Cola Company followed a year later with its first
low-calorie cola. It was given an entirely new name, Tab,
because the management held fast to its belief that the trademark "Coke" should represent only one drink. The name Tab,
in fact, came out of a computer search for a word that didn't
mean anything and that was as far as possible from any association with the mother company.

In 1964 it was Pepsi-Cola's turn to pick up the ball. They
issued diet Pepsi, which, like Tab, was sweetened with cyclamates. The two colas ran a neck-and-neck race until 1969, when
the federal government banned cyclamates because large doses
of the artificial sweetener had been found to produce cancer in
rats.

"When cyclamates were banned, everybody came back with
72-calorie diet colas, a mixture of sugar and saccharin," said
Ike Herbert. But around the same time, Coca-Cola introduced
a drink called Fresca that was sweetened only with saccharin—
and it became enormously popular.

The company surmised from the success of Fresca that people
were far more concerned about calories than about taste when
it came to selecting a diet drink. They soon issued a sugar-free
Tab, sweetened with saccharin. "It took off," said Herbert,
"even though taste tests showed the competition's sugar/
saccharin colas were preferred eighty to twenty over Tab." Tab
quickly became the number-one diet cola, and it held its lead

for twelve years, even as the other diet drinks picked up the beat with 100 percent saccharin-sweetened drinks.

But in 1975 Pepsi introduced a second diet cola, this one called Pepsi Light. Its "distinctive lemon taste," as the advertisements intoned, made an instantaneous hit. And although Tab held its top position, the combination of diet Pepsi and Pepsi Light gave the Pepsi-Cola Company the overall corporate market leadership in the diet-cola category.

So there the Coca-Cola Company sat, with the world's most famous name in soft drinks, hamstrung by its corporate culture, which prevented it from extending that trademark to a diet drink. Such a move would almost certainly have guaranteed success as long as the drink didn't taste like vinegar.

"The idea of diet Coke had been talked about since the 1960s, and once a year ever since then," said Charles Millard, the chairman of the New York Coca-Cola Bottling Company. He remained convinced that Coke should represent a single product until 1979, when he hired Ed O'Reilly as president of New York Coke. The New York market was then, as it is now, heavily tilted in favor of diet drinks. Low-calorie drinks are twice as popular in the Big Apple as they are elsewhere in the nation. O'Reilly persuaded Millard that Coca-Cola had a weapon it was refusing to deploy—a diet cola enhanced by all the tradition and prestige the name Coke would inspire.

"We met with Keough and Dyson and made a forceful case for diet Coke," Millard said. "I don't think they were there yet, but they were shortly."

What Millard and O'Reilly didn't have to tell Coca-Cola's president and the president of Coca-Cola USA was that the diet-cola segment was growing twice as fast as the total soft-drink market. As a matter of fact, it was destined within the next decade to represent a third of total soft-drink sales. Americans were becoming health conscious to the point of a national craze. They were jogging, eating less red meat, choosing a Perrier or white wine over Scotch, and ostracizing anyone who still dared to light a cigarette. Furthermore, concern about weight was no longer an obsession only of women. Increasingly, men also wanted low-calorie soft drinks but they perceived Tab as a "woman's drink." By 1979 Keough and Dyson were convinced diet Coke was a good idea. Persuading the company was a different thing entirely.

At about that time, Sergio Zyman came to the Coca-Cola Company from the opposition, Pepsi. A brilliant, energetic young Mexican, Zyman was also irreverent about some of the things Coca-Cola held sacrosanct. For as long as anyone could remember, the word "Pepsi" had not been uttered by Coca-Cola executives. In a snobbish, perhaps subconsciously fearful way, they called it "that other cola" or simply "the competition." Zyman not only called Pepsi "Pepsi," he was even caught drinking a Pepsi Light one day in the halls of Coca-Cola USA. "Pepsi had changed the taste slightly and I was just testing it out, but you would have thought I had committed a mortal sin," remarked Zyman.

Great things were expected of Zyman, and to Dyson and Keough, this dynamo who didn't carry the baggage of Coca-Cola tradition seemed a natural as the person to propose that the company take the name Coke and strategically place it after the word "diet." In 1979 Zyman wrote a paper on the subject that came to a not-unexpected conclusion: that the diet segment of the cola market was growing much too fast for Coca-

Cola to restrict itself to Tab, and that the name Coke carried enormous selling power.

The marketing research department under Roy Stout backed up Zyman's assertion about the potential of the name Coke. In taste tests where the products were clearly identified, Tab won over diet Pepsi 52 to 48. But when the researchers poured Tab into a new can labeled "diet Coke" and tested the same people's preference, the jump was astounding. "So-called diet Coke produced a twelve-point swing in their preference," said Stout. The name was that powerful.

Despite this evidence, corporate pride was as big a hindrance to the concept of diet Coke as was Justice Holmes's writ. Executives worried that if the company did bring out diet Coke, there was no guarantee it would become the number-one diet drink. Furthermore, it might kill Tab's status as number one by stealing a large part—perhaps half—of Tab's market. If diet Coke failed to rocket to the top, the first position would probably belong to diet Pepsi, a possibility hard for Coke executives to risk.

In January 1980, Keough and Dyson went to J. Paul Austin, who was still chairman and chief executive officer at that time, and finally received permission to begin work on diet Coke. Keough and Dyson asked Zyman to head up the project. At first he declined because he didn't want to postpone taking a thirteen-week management course at Harvard University. The ambitious young man had been assured by Keough and Dyson when he joined the company that he could take the well-known course soon afterward. But Zyman also knew a good opportunity when he saw one. The successful launching of diet Coke would be a tremendous achievement and a great career coup for the man who could claim the credit. That prospect was too enticing, too rewarding, to miss. Zyman code-named the diet Coke project "Harvard" and fervidly set about writing proposals to the executives of Coca-Cola. His excitement was increasing and his plan just crystallizing when the old, unstable management had a sudden change of heart. Less than two months after getting permission for diet Coke, Zyman, Dyson, and Keough were in South America and received a shocking telegram. Austin pronounced that Project Harvard was dead.

"It was devastating, frustrating," complained Keough. And when they got back to Atlanta, Dyson wrote a blistering memo to Keough saying what a mistake it was to kill Project Harvard. Neither man was given a reason for the project's termination, and "even if I had been told," said Dyson, "it wouldn't have been a satisfactory answer."

Dyson surmised later that the company may have been afraid to link the name Coke with the diet segment, which from time to time had been troubled by ingredient issues. Saccharin, like cyclamates, was found to be potentially harmful. Dyson added that this argument was "clearly stretched . . . because using the same name for a regular and a diet drink hadn't hurt our competitor. The public knows the difference."

Millard believes that Project Harvard was stopped because Austin was suffering from Alzheimer's disease, though no one knew it at the time. Keough disagrees: "There were times, in hindsight, when Austin would say something in the morning and forget it in the afternoon. Diet Coke was not one of those instances. It was just such a big issue, and one which Austin might have tackled at age fifty. But at sixty-five, you put it off."

When Roberto Goizueta was elected president in May 1980,

the climate at Coca-Cola changed almost overnight. Even
before he assumed full responsibility as chairman, he set the
company rolling in new directions, and diet Coke was one of
them. He resurrected Project Harvard, and Zyman and Dyson
went to work. From the outset, with a new management team
taking hold, Dyson was determined that diet Coke be handled
differently than any product had been in the past. To Dyson,
different means unorthodox. Rather than automatically handing
the diet Coke advertising assignment to McCann-Erickson
(brand Coke's agency of twenty-five years), he selected SSC&B,
one of the hottest shops in New York at that time. Since both
agencies are part of the Interpublic Group, a holding company
of a number of advertising agencies, the client was still in
Interpublic's stable. (Another Interpublic agency handled the
Sprite account.)

The diet-cola marketplace had changed since the early seventies, when the company discovered that calorie count, not taste,
was the overriding consumer issue. Now consumers *assumed* a
diet drink would be low in calories. If that was a given, what
could make one diet drink sell more than any other? Taste, the
Coca-Cola officials deduced. So the new advertising slogan
heralded a new taste sensation: "Just for the taste of it, diet
Coke." But the last word of the slogan probably had the most
impact of all.

Although the company never tested diet Coke in any market
prior to its introduction, Roy Stout's marketing-research department did plenty of experiments with consumers to determine
how much diet Coke would interest them and how much it
would "cannibalize," or take away from, the sales of Tab and
Coke.

Since the late 1960s, Stout had been testing consumers' preference for new products with his own "purchase intent" game, using poker chips and simulated grocery-store aisles. The game is set up in shopping malls, where shoppers are solicited to "play" consumer. Stout's research team erects a replica of a grocery store aisle stocked with soft drinks. Each player receives ten poker chips that will "buy" any of the drinks. The players are instructed to think about their entire household when they make decisions about what their next ten purchases should be. In other words, they should consider the likes and needs of the whole family and not simply buy for themselves. "If a player is a housewife, for example," said Stout, "she might purchase her children's favorite soft drinks weekly, but for her husband, who might not drink as many, she might buy some drinks every other week. And the same for herself."

The poker-chip tests, which Stout believes are a very realistic model of people's purchasing patterns, were "phenomenally accurate" in predicting consumer interest in a diet Coke. But further testing also accurately forecasted the cannibalization effect.

This time two aisles were built in a mall. One offered the array of soft drinks then on the market; the other contained the same drinks but also cans and bottles labeled "diet Coke." Stout's team asked the participants to "shop" the first aisle, using their ten poker chips. Then, with ten more chips, they shopped the second aisle, which contained diet Coke among the choices. If someone chose diet Coke, it was relatively simple to ascertain, from looking at his selections in the first aisle, which drink he was now passing up in favor of diet Coke.

This test led Coca-Cola's management to predict that 30

percent of diet Coke's volume would come from brand Coke and 15 percent would come from Tab.

It took two years of plodding, plotting, and continued debate over the trademark and the effect of a diet Coke on the company's other products, but in mid-1982, Coca-Cola was ready to introduce diet Coke.

By that time, however, the soft-drink industry had come up with a new marketing gimmick—caffeine-free drinks. The 7-Up Company, which had yet to make a profit for its owners, the Philip Morris Company, was capitalizing on the concern over caffeine with its "Never had it, never will" advertising campaign. Royal Crown was doing reasonably well with its two caffeine-free colas, RC 100 and RC 100 regular, the latter containing sugar. And in July 1982, Pepsi-Cola announced two caffeine-free versions of its flagship brand, dubbed Pepsi Free and Sugar-free Pepsi.

Coca-Cola steered clear of the caffeine debate and then blindsided the competition with diet Coke. Though the new drink contained caffeine, that wasn't an issue. As it turned out, the question of caffeine or no caffeine was never to have much effect on sales of the various brands.

In August 1982, Coca-Cola introduced diet Coke in New York with all the fanfare the company could muster. The commercial that launched the new drink was one of the most expensive in the company's history, costing $1.5 million to produce. Titled "Premiere," it featured the Rockettes hoofing it in front of a giant Coke can as celebrities like Bob Hope, Joe Namath, Carol Channing, Ben Vereen, Telly Savalas, Glenn Ford, Susan Anton, Sally Kellerman, and Robert Vaughn pulled up at Radio City Music Hall in chauffeured limousines.

By the end of 1983 diet Coke was the best-selling *diet* drink in the United States, and by 1984 it was the number-three soft drink overall, replacing 7-Up in the ranking. It trailed only Pepsi, number two, and Coke, number one. The beverage world agreed with Coca-Cola's boast that diet Coke was the most successful new product introduced in the history of the beverage industry. And when you combine diet Coke and Tab sales, the Coca-Cola Company as a corporation had achieved market-share leadership.

Diet Coke's victory was not without its problems, however. When the diet cola was introduced, the company required most of its U.S. bottlers to sign special diet Coke contracts that set a higher price for the syrup than the cost of regular Coke syrup. In March 1983, a group of eighteen small Coca-Cola bottlers sued the Coca-Cola Company, contending that their original contract entitled them to the rights of the names "Coke" and "Coca-Cola," and that diet Coke was merely a modified formula of Coke. Therefore, they argued, bottlers should get diet Coke syrup at the regular Coke price. The suit is still pending.

For the most part, though, Coca-Cola was enjoying its successes. In 1983, no longer timid, the company issued not just one new brand but caffeine-free versions of Coke, diet Coke, and Tab. With his usual self-confidence Dyson predicted that Coke's new caffeine-free colas would gain half of the caffeine-free cola market by 1984. In the end, the drinks didn't live up to those expectations, but the people at Coca-Cola still were riding high, ready for any challenge.

Indeed, hubris was in the air at the Coca-Cola Company. The new management team had been more than right about the purchase of Columbia Pictures, which quickly became one of the jewels in the crown. And almost as important as Columbia's financial contribution to the company was the reversal of the criticism that the purchase had initially produced. The collective management was vindicated. Coca-Cola could and did say, "We told you so." Adding to their confidence was diet Coke's undisputed success, achieved far sooner than even its advocates at Coca-Cola had anticipated.

The marketing axiom "Ready, fire, aim" was fast becoming the battle cry of these men. They were responding to the marketplace and to their competitors with speed and an aggressiveness heretofore unknown in what once had been a stodgy company. The press was impressed and so was Wall Street.

On Sunday, March 4, 1984, the business section of the *New York Times* chronicled this new Coca-Cola Company under the headline "Putting the Daring Back in Coke." It credited Roberto Goizueta with most of the company's recent changes and successes. The chairman, in turn, made one of the more prophetic statements of his career: "There is a danger when a company is doing as well as we are. And that is, to think that we can do no wrong."

Behind the good news, Goizueta knew, there was one nagging problem to contend with—the declining market share and slowing volume growth of the drink the company was founded on and named for, Coca-Cola itself. In 1984, working on that situation became top management's top priority.

CHAPTER 8
PROJECT KANSAS

Soaring pride and comfortable profits in 1984 made it very difficult for Coca-Cola's top officials to accept that as Coke—the beverage itself—neared its hundredth birthday its lead over Pepsi was decreasing fast. Market tests confirmed what diminishing growth suggested: Coke's tight-fisted hold on the U.S. market share of soft drinks in the mid-fifties, when it outsold Pepsi better than two to one, had crumbled to a mere 4.9 percent lead by 1984. And in the grocery-store market America's favorite was now *trailing* by 1.7 percent.

Yet Coca-Cola spent far more than Pepsi on advertising. It was competitively priced and was more widely distributed than Pepsi. Apparently marketing technique was not the crux of the problem. In the end company executives had no choice but to consider the product itself. When they did that, the evidence they'd been collecting themselves as well as that of the Pepsi

Challenge made them conclude that taste had to be the single most important cause of Coke's decline.

Even so, it would not be an easy task to lift the sacred mantle from the product on which the company's pride was founded. Indeed, for a long time top management chose to ignore the numbers and statistics painstakingly gathered by Roy Stout and his marketing-research department. Stout looks almost professorial with graying hair and heavy-lidded eyes—as if he would be more comfortable in tweeds or a coat with leather-patched elbows than in the pin-striped executive uniform typical of Coca-Cola culture—but he is scarcely sleepy or retiring. With a Ph.D. in economics from North Carolina State University, he joined Coca-Cola in 1967 and rose rapidly to become manager of a new management-science department in 1972. Three years later, when his department merged with the marketing-research department, Stout took control of that vitally important branch of the company. His clout at Coca-Cola was such that on one occasion he blocked a commercial that had cost $750,000 to produce before it was ever aired on TV, because his research had indicated that it wasn't just right.

As early as 1976 Stout had compiled a top-secret report, including computer printouts, charts, and graphs, that showed significant leadership over Pepsi was no longer a given. Though that information was largely ignored, Stout's report did make some executives extremely jittery, and it was *not even shown* to the board of directors.

Stout claimed that in 1972, 18 percent of soft-drink users were exclusive Coke drinkers while a mere 4 percent drank only Pepsi. Ten years later, only 12 percent claimed total loyalty to

Coke and a close 11 percent now said they chose Pepsi exclusively.

Some suggested that Coke's greater availability was a reason —and a tenuous one—for Coke's continued lead. Stout said that Coke had a higher share of sales than of preference, meaning that fewer people said they liked Coke best than "share-of-the-market" figures reflected. With Pepsi, the opposite was true: those who favored Pepsi represented in theory a greater number of people than was indicated by Pepsi's market share. The discrepancy, said Stout, arose from the fact that even if someone *wanted* Pepsi, he might in some places *only find Coke*. Everyone at Coca-Cola knew that in the coming years that situation would change, and the result was too shocking to imagine.

Since 1976 Stout's department had been using a complicated formula to try to measure the effect of advertising on sales. It came up with an Advertising Pressure Index, based on a score established by an outside research firm grading the quality of both Coke's and Pepsi's advertising. This figure was multiplied by the amount of money spent airing the ads, and then by the "promotional index," a complicated formula that weighed the influence of devices like newspaper coupons. The results were as complicated to evaluate as the methods, but they seemed to indicate that no matter how much money Coca-Cola poured into its marketing programs, the results were not significant enough. "We estimated that the system, including bottlers and the company annually outspent Pepsi by $100 million, and still our share declined," said Stout. "In 1980, when we grew share [slightly] versus Pepsi, we outspent them by $150 million."

If the *amount* of advertising wasn't the thing to tip the scales, was it the *quality*? Was Pepsi's promotion, with its sensational Pepsi Generation theme, simply more effective? Many experts acknowledged that it was, but even hardcore proponents of advertising had to admit that advertising alone couldn't account for Pepsi's aggressive advance, or Coke's devastating decline.

Stout asked top management, "If we have twice as many vending machines, dominate fountain, have more shelf space, spend more on advertising, and are competitively priced, why are we losing share?" His case was getting harder and harder for management to ignore. "You look at the Pepsi Challenge," he insisted, "and you have to begin asking about taste."

Brian Dyson, who had become president of Coca-Cola USA in 1978, was one executive who was willing to address that issue and analyze why the universal appeal of Coca-Cola's taste was sadly slipping. "Maybe the principal characteristics that made Coke distinctive, like its bite, consumers now describe as harsh. And when you mention words like 'rounded' and 'smooth,' they say 'Pepsi.' Maybe the way we assuage our thrist has changed."

But for nearly one hundred years, the taste of Coke had not changed. Its well-known kick had remained exactly the same, even as flavor technology advanced and people's tastes and habits changed. Almost every other consumer product had been revamped and touted as "new and improved." Even Pepsi had changed its taste on a couple of occasions. But not Coke, not once.

As Dyson reviewed the graphs depicting the archrivals' claims on total market share over the past years, he saw Pepsi creeping relentlessly toward Coke. If that trend continued, he realized, it would soon surpass the king of colas and perhaps stay ahead forever. "I'm not going to sit on my ass and watch that," he avowed. "To do nothing means that I am forever condemned to not touching my product even though I know I can make a better product and move with consumer tastes. To do nothing means you're locked out of doing what you do for every other product. Goddammit, if I do nothing I can't keep my product modern, and eventually anything that doesn't change in the face of change will wither and die—that's the law of nature."

Dyson was faced with a dilemma and he approached it head-on. "You can't look at your lead product and not ask whether or not taste is an issue," he asserted. "Coke didn't win the sip tests. On sip tests, Pepsi was validated, and taste, over time, must play a role. You can't ignore it. If you want to be the leading brand, you can't have a taste disadvantage that is proclaimable."

By early 1983 Dyson and Stout began taking their case to the senior executives of Coca-Cola. Ironically, that same year the Pepsi-Cola Company discontinued the Pepsi Challenge, because of a change in management and a decision to return to a campaign emphasizing Pepsi's image and that of its users. But the men from Pepsi certainly didn't ease up on the pressure they were applying to their stodgy nemesis. In 1983 they signed Michael Jackson, the sensational singer and teenage idol, to a $5 million endorsement contract to help resurrect the Pepsi Generation with "Pepsi, the Choice of a New Generation." Not long before, Coca-Cola had turned down Michael Jackson as a candidate for its advertising because he was considered too flashy and his androgynous appearance didn't jibe with the company's image of the all-American boy.

When Don Keough heard about the radical move that Stout

and Dyson were advancing, his instinctive reaction was negative. Keough is probably one of the smartest marketers leading
a consumer-goods company today. He'd seen Stout's charts, he
knew that the sugar-cola category of soft drinks, which accounted for 60 percent of his company's volume, was deteriorat-
ing, and he understood full well that some action had to be
taken. Still, he balked, delivering a stern lecture to Dyson and
Stout about how the public and press would react if they did
meddle with the taste of Coke, which was as American as the
flag. After it was all over, looking back at the torrent of evidence in favor of change, Keough was to confess that those
original instinctive feelings "got lost in my mind."

Indeed, Dyson and his team at Coca-Cola USA barraged the
Tower in Atlanta with all the ammunition Stout's research could
supply. By the fall of 1983 top management gave the go-ahead
"to explore the possibility of a reformulation."

Dyson immediately chose Sergio Zyman to head the project.
Although Zyman had been with the company only four and a
half years, he had been vice-president of bottler operations,
director of fountain sales, Keough's executive assistant, and
was now senior vice-president of marketing Coca-Cola USA.
He had directed McCann-Erickson's work on the 1982 advertising slogan "Coke is it!" and he claimed responsibility for the
success of diet Coke. Indisputably on the fast track, Zyman had
acquired an unfortunate reputation for overzealousness among
some who worked with him. But single-minded leadership and
dauntless confidence were precisely the qualities that would be
needed to steer the corporation from its traditionally conservative course.

In September 1983, Zyman became manager of the new experiment. Its code name was first Zeus, then Tampa, then Eton and finally Project Kansas, after an article by William Allen White in the Emporia *Gazette* of Emporia, Kansas: "Coca-Cola is the sublimated essence of all that America stands for. A decent thing, honestly made, universally distributed and conscientiously improved with the years." It was one of Robert Woodruff's favorite quotes.

For about a year, Project Kansas consisted of a very small group of no more than fourteen people. Zyman took a special office on the twenty-fifth floor of the Tower, where, for security reasons, he worked alone on his word processor, without a secretary, and all memoranda ended up in the paper shredder.

Perhaps because of his foreign background, perhaps because he was relatively new to the scene at Coca-Cola, Zyman had little problem with the idea of changing the century-old taste. And he was quick to accuse reluctant managers of inability to act with the times. "They couldn't equate logical, rational business processes to Coke," he remarked. "They didn't want to hear that Coke had lost its relevance. They didn't want to hear that word." In fact Zyman knew that for years Stout had been producing data for top executives that they had refused to consider. Even now, even among the chosen few in the Projcet Kansas group, there was dissent about how far the company should go. Some felt the taste should be "improved a little bit," some thought the company should issue two Cokes, and others wanted a "balls to the wall" move—replace the old favorite with a new Coke and a new taste. Uprooting the old loyalty was a challenge even to powerhouse Zyman.

"It was hard to get people to understand that values had changed. 'Refreshing' and 'thirst-quenching' were no longer the reason you bought a particular soft drink, no longer a benefit—it was a given and the cost of entry," Zyman said. "But taste had become very important because of the Pepsi Challenge."

Although these discussions and initial preparations for re-formulations were under way, Coca-Cola's technical department still hadn't concocted a formula that could beat Pepsi. In the absence of an accepted formula to test-market, Roy Stout concentrated on testing the *idea* of a change in Coke. This process, which had been going on for some years, was a complex and delicate business designed to keep the company's real intentions a secret. In 1980 Stout's department tested one of the many trial products on a group of two hundred households said to be heavy soft-drinker users. The new product was put in the regular Coke bottle and two cases of it were shipped to each family. They were told only that the Coke had been "processed differently." The response was not rebellion but overwhelming approval. In the next test, another group of heavy users was given a case of the "new" Coke and one of Pepsi, while a control group was provided with Pepsi and the new Coke but were led to believe it was regular old Coke. Stout's team discovered that those who knew they were drinking the "new-process" Coke preferred it to Pepsi, but the control group, which thought it was drinking old Coke, selected Pepsi. The results indicated to Stout's department that there would be tolerance of a change in Coca-Cola.

In 1982 the Coca-Cola Company conducted two thousand interviews in ten major markets to investigate further the public's willingness to accept a different Coke. Consumers were shown storyboards, comic-striplike mock commercials. One board said Coke had added a new ingredient and it tasted smoother, while another said the same about Pepsi. (To compensate for the impact of first impressions, one thousand people were shown the Coke statement first and the other one thousand saw the Pepsi announcement first.) Then Coca-Cola asked the consumers a long series of questions about what their reactions to such a change would be. Would you be upset? Would you try the new drink? Would you switch brands immediately? "We estimated from the response that ten to twelve percent of exclusive Coke drinkers would be upset, and that half of those would get over it, but half wouldn't," said Stout.

More important to Coca-Cola at that time was the discovery from these interviews that exclusive Pepsi drinkers would be interested in a new Coke. Over the years, the exclusive Pepsi drinker had always rated Pepsi higher than exclusive Coke drinkers rated Coke. Worse still, Coke drinkers rated Pepsi higher than Pepsi drinkers rated Coke, which meant Coke drinkers were less loyal and easier to persuade to switch. Even in Coca-Cola's heartland, Coke won over Pepsi by only five or ten points, whereas in areas like Philadelphia, Pittsburgh, Cleveland, and Detroit, Pepsi was favored by a far greater margin—as much as forty points in some cities. The new findings about Pepsi drinkers were therefore surprising and encouraging.

While the interviews pointed to people's willingness to try a new Coke, Zyman and Stout discovered through other tests that many people just didn't believe anyone could or should tamper with the king of the colas. To hear debate on the issue, Coca-Cola's research department used focus groups, a favorite marketing tool. A focus group consists of a small number of people solicited through independent research firms and paid a nominal fee to discuss a product under the guidance of a moderator. The client, in this case Coca-Cola, usually views the proceedings through a one-way mirror.

Some of Stout's focus groups were shown storyboards depicting a proposed commercial. One said Brand X soft drink was going to be improved. "Fine," the group replied, and they were equally sanguine about a proposed improvement in Pepsi. But when it came to changing Coke for the better, the resounding response was *NO*. "It was like saying you were going to make the flag prettier," said Zyman. A similar response came in 1983 from a group that included some exclusive Coke drinkers. This group agreed that Anheuser-Busch could change Budweiser but in no way should the Coca-Cola Company try to improve Coke.

In other focus groups Zyman and Stout witnessed a recurring problem. When asked, "What is your favorite drink?," most people exclaimed, "Coke!" When asked, "What do you drink?," the response was a bit more vague—sometimes Coke, sometimes Pepsi, maybe even Brand X if it was on sale. There appeared to be a disturbing gap between what people *said* and what they *did*. Stout wondered if Coke had become an idea that everyone took for granted rather than a product they were committed to buying to the exclusion of all others.

In the end, then, some of the focus groups had revealed considerable resistance to a change in the taste of Coke, but others had disclosed a willingness to choose another drink upon occasion. So the technical division persisted in its efforts to brew up a Coke that would be more pleasing than Pepsi and that would arouse the public with a taste that could not be ignored.

In September 1984, they said they had it. Stout was skeptical at first, having seen so many new formulas fail in tests against the competitor, but this time his initial research produced astounding results. In blind taste-tests the new formula beat Pepsi by a margin of six to eight points, whereas Pepsi had hammered old Coke by anywhere from ten to fifteen points in earlier tests.

"That's an eighteen-point swing," Stout declared. Still more mind-boggling were results showing that Pepsi drinkers who previously chose Pepsi over Coke something like seventy to thirty in blind taste-tests now picked new Coke 50 percent of the time.

This was the news Dyson had been waiting for, the end of the nightmare in which Pepsi became number one. "The minute we had the product, Coca-Cola USA said let's set it in motion," recalled Dyson. He was absolutely convinced that the company had to forge ahead with the new formula, even though "things might happen we couldn't anticipate." For the president of Coca-Cola USA, it was enough to know that the company was finally going to address a critical problem, finally had a solution in hand.

Thrilled with the new product, Dyson and Zyman wanted rapid, decisive action from the Tower, but the response was ambivalent. Sure, the executives were glad to have a product that upstaged Pepsi, but now what were they going to do with it? Some executives pointed out that Coca-Cola's product line was already unwieldly and bottlers would not be happy about adding yet another cola to the list. Others believed that the tests were so convincing that the company should simply introduce a second Coke. But Stout, Dyson, and Zyman were afraid that move would only exacerbate the problems with the flag-ship brand and hasten its decline by cutting into its market. However, Stout's department did no actual research measuring whether Coca-Cola should introduce a line extension of Coke. They therefore never tested to what extent a new cola would pirate the sales of old Coke.

Another factor was clouding the issue: if this new Coke was indeed better than old Coke, you could not have it out there at the same time as old faithful, inviting invidious comparison. The trademark Coke had to be the best-tasting cola in the world.

There was concern over the fountain business, too. "If we do a new Coke and it tastes better than Coke, does McDonald's go with the new one?" asked Charles Millard.* It would certainly damage Coke's image to have McDonald's choose the new taste when old Coke was still out there as an option. Millard added, "In 1984, the company decided that the best product had to bear the name Coke—a fair conclusion reached emotionally, but there was corporate heritage involved."

"Whether that question of two Cokes was evaluated enough, no one will ever know," Millard later said, "but the thinking was that we could not be in the position of having our flagship brand not be number one in taste." Millard said it was this argument that truly won the day. Zyman also believes that an obsession with being number one in *all* phases ruled out the idea of a second cola. Two Cokes would most likely split Coke's market share and Pepsi would become the number-one soft drink, an intolerable situation for Coca-Cola.

---

* Ironically, in 1986, McDonald's was to switch from new Coke back to old, the opposite of what the company was worried about.

As the winter of 1984 approached, Dyson's men at Coca-Cola USA brought all pressure to bear against the management in the Tower. They needed a decision fast if they were going to get the new drink on the market in time for the summer season, when soft-drink consumption peaks. Also, since researchers had warned Dyson that there would be flak from about 5 percent of the most loyal Coke drinkers, he wanted time to calm them down before the centennial celebration in 1986. If a new Coke was to be introduced, he thought, it had to be done in 1985 or delayed for two long years.

Until this time Keough had distanced himself from Project Kansas, anticipating the stormy public outcry he believed was sure to follow any change in the taste of Coke. But he couldn't disregard Coke's market-share decline or Stout's taste tests, which continued to show new Coke winning out over old Coke and Pepsi by margins that were staggering. By late 1984, Keough said, "My own data bank made it easy to proceed." A rational decision based on facts had superseded his gut reaction against toying with America's heritage.

During the holiday lull of 1984, when most people were recovering from year-end festivities, four men met to decide the fate of Coca-Cola. Goizueta, Herbert, Dyson, and Keough voted and unanimously agreed to give Coke a new taste.

On January 4, 1981, sixteen men walked a labyrinthine indoor route from the offices of the McCann-Erickson advertising agency at 485 Lexington Avenue in New York to an adjoining building, home of the Interpublic Group of advertising agencies, at 750 Third Avenue. Only two of the sixteen knew the purpose of the top-secret meeting. It was held in an isolated fourth-floor room that was normally the office of account-

ants, and at the door, a specially hired Pinkerton guard
checked the IDs of each senior executive. They then entered a
U-shaped room furnished sparsely with what looked like army-
issue tables, desks, and chairs. Along the back wall of the room
were four small offices—the only privacy that would be provided to this creative team. Six cubicles ran down the middle
and around the right side of the room. The left side was the
conference room, which had been turned into an audiovisual
center of TV sets, video-cassette recorders, video screens, tape
players, flip charts, and a T-shaped table. A paper shredder
stood near the only exit, a constant reminder that no scrap was
to leave the room. The effect was far closer to an underground
military command post than to the plush offices in Manhattan
high-rise buildings that these highly paid top-level advertising
people were used to. In fact the meeting place was later referred
to as "the bunker."

The leaders of the meeting were Ike Herbert, Coca-Cola's
executive vice-president and director of corporate marketing,
and Sergio Zyman, vice-president of marketing for Coca-Cola
USA. Here, safely concealed from the public and the press and
even their own staff, they announced with confidence, "We're
replacing Coke with a new Coke." John Bergin, the president of
McCann-Erickson U.S.A., and the other advertising men in the
room were absolutely stunned.

McCann-Erickson had expected to hear that their client was
going to introduce a "flanker" cola, which would stand proudly
beside the Coke brand as an alternative taste. Many in the room
had been advocating that strategy for quite a while. Some had
proposed a cola with fewer calories than regular Coke, one

containing a blend of sugar and the noncaloric aspartame NutraSweet. Others endorsed a sweeter auxiliary Coke aimed to win some of the younger consumers who had been drinking Pepsi's sweeter cola. The admen had even gone as far as to dream up names for a flanker brand, such as Coke Two. Coke 100, also a possible name, was intended to correlate with the company's upcoming hundredth anniversary.

Although the admen were shocked at the news, they weren't given much opportunity to debate it. "We weren't asking their opinion on *whether* to do it, but *how* to do it," Herbert said. The decision to alter the taste that had endured for ninety-nine years had been firmly sealed at the highest levels of the Coca-Cola Company just days before.

Herbert assigned to the advertising men the complex task of developing the most effective way to tell the world about the new taste of Coke. Time was short. Atlanta had chosen late April as a launch date. Until then, Herbert stressed, secrecy was of paramount importance. If the real purpose of Project Kansas leaked, the company would have to proceed even before the bottlers were informed and before advertising, packaging design, and press-conference plans were ready, and the result could be catastrophic. Herbert didn't have to mention that a leak would also give Pepsi-Cola advance warning of its enemy's most daring assault ever in the cola wars. "If it leaks and we trace it to you, you're fired," Herbert told members of the group, the new initiates in Project Kansas.

On January 14 Dyson issued confidential memos to ten Coca-Cola executives *ordering* them to attend a meeting the following week in the Coca-Cola USA building, next door to the Tower.

One of the recipients of the unusual note was Carlton Curtis, the director of corporate communications for Coca-Cola. A bright young man who has never worked for another company, Curtis epitomizes Coca-Cola. He dresses for success in pin-striped suits and starched shirts, his hair always neatly cut. He is patient, articulate, and quick to assimilate the company line. Curtis thought it odd to get a memo from Dyson, as he usually dealt with the executives in the Tower. The date of the meeting —Martin Luther King Jr.'s birthday—was strange too, since the company had decided to celebrate it as a holiday, although it would not be made a national holiday until the following year.

At the meeting Curtis found the heads of Coca-Cola's packaging, research, bottling, merchandising, and fountain operations. He attended such big meetings day in and day out, but he sensed right away that this one was different—everyone felt "something truly significant was about to happen." Dyson took control and, much like a college professor, led the class through the recent history of Coke, focusing on the weakening of its position as the undisputed king of colas. He told the group about the possibility of the company's issuing a new flavor for Coke, but "the entire project was couched as a hypothetical situation," said Curtis; even so, they were all sworn to secrecy. Within a week, the hypothetical situation became all too real as these men were presented with an enormously complex assignment. They would have to plan, down to the minutest detail, how best to inform the bottlers, securities analysts, shareholders, media, and the public about Coke's new taste. They would have to say the same thing to everyone and say it all at the same time, a dizzying feat of coordination.

There followed almost daily discussions between Curtis, Keough, Goizueta, Herbert and a few others about how to position new Coke, how to handle the press, and how to place the announcement in the best possible light. Curtis's boss, Garth Hamby, the executive vice-president of administration, and Earl Leonard, senior vice-president of public affairs, were also privy to these furtive debates. The toughest question they knew the media, shareholders, and consumers would ask was "If it ain't broke, why fix it?" It was a question they could never answer to the satisfaction of those who asked, because to be blunt and truthful about Coke's cracked façade was for many reasons not a "viable alternative," said Curtis.

Coca-Cola's corporate culture, with its massive ego, wouldn't allow the company to admit publicly that Pepsi was in any way superior. "The system couldn't get itself to say that Pepsi tasted better than Coke," said Goizueta. And the chairman couldn't even tell the press that in taste tests, new Coke beat Pepsi, because "the concern was that someone would then ask how old Coke did versus Pepsi." Ironically, by not being more candid about taste, Coca-Cola succeeded in making it the focal issue. But instead of comparing new Coke with Pepsi, the public would respond by judging new Coke against old Coke. "That became the issue, and we created it," Goizueta admitted later.

At the time there were several other reasons why full disclosure of old Coke's problems was not feasible. Such openness would have upset loyal Coke drinkers and supplied Pepsi with an arsenal of valuable information. "And then the person who had recommended that candid approach would have been blamed," Curtis said. "It would have been hard to advocate that approach."

Coca-Cola was committed to perpetuating the image of a vital product that was an integral part of American life, an image, however illusory, that reflected the very soul of the company. "We were not going to launch a new product by trouncing on Coke," said Curtis. "We weren't going to damage the name Coke, which is a bigger thing than just a formula." In much of the world Coke continued to hold commanding share leads over Pepsi, and the company wasn't about to tell those markets that Pepsi actually tasted better, that it was a viable alternative, that suddenly Coca-Cola wasn't all that it should be.

Coca-Cola decided to let the industry observers shoulder the burden of informing the public about those unpleasant matters. "The assumption was that we could soft-pedal the harsh reality as an official position," said Curtis. "The market share numbers were well known by industry analysts, who would lay it out . . . to the press, which in turn would inform the public."

As Project Kansas gained momentum, Coca-Cola executives tried to anticipate the public's reaction and mold their new publicity campaign accordingly. One of the cardinal rules, first laid down by Herbert in the bunker, was never, never apply the word "new" to the new Coke, because it would denote too drastic a change. After all, "We weren't turning it into orange soda," reasoned Herbert. Backed by Keough and Goizueta, he advocated a simple redesign of the can to introduce the slightly different product. But Coca-Cola USA didn't agree, and neither did many of the bottlers. Research from focus groups had shown that the word "new" generated the biggest and quickest response. And many Coca-Cola executives, including Herbert and Goizueta, actually feared that their announcement would be met with a yawn, that the public would say, "So what?" That prospect was too much for Goizueta to bear. "I caved in," he admitted later, acknowledging that the company had made a major mistake by calling the new Coke "new."

The Kansas team at this time was forging ahead with consumer testing. Since the fall of 1984, when results had revealed that Coca-Cola had a better-tasting cola than old Coke and Pepsi, Stout's department had continued to verify the preference for the new taste. They checked with different age groups in various parts of the country, and their findings remained similar to those of the first tests. But there was a rather significant oversight. Although earlier studies had shown that 10 to 12 percent of exclusive Coke drinkers would be upset over any new taste for their favorite, the researchers predicted half of those would get over it. "But the other half wouldn't," Stout said, and the tests for this group were inadequate. Incredible as it seems in retrospect, the researchers never made it clear to the consumers they tested that old Coke would not be around as a choice, whether or not they liked new Coke. So the marketers never ascertained the range of emotions the removal of old Coke would elicit, nor did they pursue questions that would have helped the company manage the outrage. "That was a mistake," Stout admitted, and Zyman echoed him, saying that "maybe we goofed" in not stressing in the tests that this new taste would *replace* the old one, that Coke as everyone knew it would disappear. In fairness, however, it would have been hard to get at this point without giving the secret plan away.

Interestingly, however, at about this time, Ike Herbert did say that if the small band of old-Coke loyalists protested long enough, the company could *reissue* old Coke in time for the centennial, in mid-1986, after new Coke had had ample time to establish itself in the marketplace. It was not considered at all likely that this would happen, however.

In January and February Stout and his team were actually testing two versions of new Coke, one exactly as sweet as Pepsi, the other slightly sweeter. In taste tests against Pepsi both new Cokes won. "It was hard to detect a preference," said Stout, "but if you wanted to look at certain numbers a certain way, you could make a case that a sweeter taste may have had a half-point to a one-point preference. The thinking was that if Coca-Cola came out with a cola with a sweetness parity with Pepsi, then Pepsi could easily make theirs sweeter without their loyalists detecting a real difference." For this reason, Dyson, Zyman, and Stout opted for the sweeter taste at the very time when Coca-Cola commercials on TV featured Bill Cosby praising Coke for being *less* sweet than Pepsi. The timing was unfortunate to say the least.

The commercials in which Cosby knocked the rival's sugary sweetness were the brainchild of Sergio Zyman, who had had some trouble getting the company to endorse the advertising ploy. The idea was conceived in 1983, before the decision to issue new Coke, and the commercials began airing in October 1984, though on a trial basis. They were intended to run mainly in Pepsi heartland, but as often happens with such localized promotions, bottlers elsewhere began demanding the commercial. "It got away from us," said Ike Herbert. "We never intended for it to be a national campaign." Zyman was quick to point out that the ads helped boost Coke's image for the first time in years, but they certainly wouldn't help new Coke. As Herbert put it, "The campaign got out of hand, and bit us in the ass."

"Sweetness became the biggest negative" for new Coke, said Stout. Though the nation would rise up to debate sweetness, "the sweetness brouhaha was a surprise to us," Herbert said. He also admitted that he didn't even know new Coke had more calories than old Coke until the company's rehearsal for the press conference in April. The blowup would be all the more exasperating since the difference in sweetness was so infinitesimal. "We are only talking about a difference of a few calories, for God's sake," snapped Herbert. And Stout added that there was "hardly a noticeable difference, but . . . Pepsi exploited the hell out of it." In fact, a six-ounce serving of new Coke had only five more calories than old Coke and *fewer* calories than Pepsi—even though it was sweeter.

The technical division had made not only a sweeter Coke but also a smoother one. "People told us they didn't like the bite of Coke," said Stout, so the company concentrated on correcting it. Coca-Cola didn't purposely decide to make a flat cola, but that's what they wound up with—at least compared with *old* Coke it was flat. And Stout later said, "New Coke was more different from old Coke, more than I realized at the time."

Zyman blamed the technical people for not bringing both these taste issues to the company's attention before the product was released. "They just kept saying it was better," he said. Stout, on the other hand, says that top executives knew from the start exactly how the taste would change. Probably the explanation is that the management team was chafing at the bit to hit the marketplace with a new Coke and was all too ready to put aside any reservations.

Throughout the winter of 1985, Project Kansas was growing. This expansion was essential but it only aggravated the company's fear that the news would leak prematurely. Some new members, therefore, weren't told the whole story. Some didn't really know why they were given a particular assignment, such as the artists who were asked to conceive a new design for a special Coke can, supposedly to celebrate good old Coca-Cola on the company's hundredth anniversary. Another company strategy was to instigate false rumors to keep the press off the scent. One container manufacturer was supplied with artwork for a Coke with "20% fewer calories," while rumors abounded about a new Minute Maid orange soda.

A very real and very convenient cover turned out to be cherry Coke (Coke containing cherry syrup), which had been mixed at drugstore soda fountains for decades. Along with Stout's hundreds of tests on new Coke, he had also found time to evaluate cherry Coke. His poker-chip game in the simulated supermarket aisles showed cherry Coke to be most promising, so promising that in February 1985 New York Coke demanded permission to test-market the drink against USA's wishes. Almost immediately, bottlers across the country clamored for cherry Coke, and the product flew. By the end of the year some market researchers ranked it as tied for tenth place in the soft-drink market. It was a new feather in Coca-Cola's cap, an achievement nearly as successful as diet Coke, and a well-timed distraction for the beverage industry and the media tracking Coca-Cola's moves.

While the Project Kansas team scrambled to prepare for the debut of new Coke, they had to keep on publicizing old Coke as well. Eight new TV spots appeared in February, updating the "Coke is it!" theme with contemporary music and defining "it" with new lyrics: "It's a kiss, a glance, it is hot, it is cool . . . it's a kick, it's a hit, it's a Coke. Coke is it!" They also stubbornly continued the Cosby ads that promoted the "less sweet, real cola taste" of Coke. The rationale for this strange decision? If it's working, keep using it—despite the imminent launch of a *very* sweet Coke.

Behind the scenes the admen of McCann-Erickson were sweating under an excruciating deadline and, worse, were in disagreement about what to do with new Coke. Committees never create good advertising, says an old advertising axiom, and the group that met time and again in the bunker was no exception. The "horrendous committee meetings," as Zyman said, produced nothing for weeks on end. He and Herbert finally formed two groups to work independently and, they hoped, more efficiently. Zyman and Bergin, the president of McCann-Erickson, were by then on less than friendly terms. Bergin worked alone, while Zyman boarded the Concorde, bound for London to make his commercials there. After an exhausting few weeks of transatlantic flights he was ready, and a skeleton crew shot twenty-seven Cosby spots in three days, with Zyman himself writing and rewriting as they went along. One such spot figured Cosby, dressed in a drab gray tunic, standing in front of some imitations of ancient Roman busts. With all the presumption he could muster he declared: "The words I'm about to say will change the course of history. Coca-Cola has a new taste and it's the best-tasting Coca-Cola ever.

You like Coke the way it is? Me too. Always did. I like this one better. . . . You're a Pepsi drinker? Ah well, maybe that'll be history too after you try the new taste of Coke. Now, more than ever, 'Coke is it.' "

Meanwhile, in New York, the admen were creating and debating some new theme lines for new Coke such as "It's all right here," "Going one better," and "We've got a taste for you." But nothing hit home, nothing stuck, nothing leaped out as a surefire sensation. In the end, they lapsed back into the old time-tested favorite, "I'd like to teach the world to sing." An adaptation of this song was combined with the lyrics for "Coke is it!" just issued in February, but the result was ineffective and unexciting, simply not spectacular enough to support the replacement of America's favorite soft drink. "My feeling," said Herbert, "was that we should have come out with a whole new campaign and new music, but we were a victim of our own time frame."

Yet another part of the admen's job was to anticipate what Pepsi would have to say about new Coke. A group was asked to prepare examples of Pepsi's retaliatory promotion. One ad showed consumers who couldn't tell the difference between new and old Coke. Another asserted that old Coke was better but that it wasn't around anymore. Another asked the question Why has Coke changed? In response, a consumer holds up a Pepsi can and asks rhetorically, "Which one is the real thing?" The idea of Pepsi declaring itself "the real, real thing" scared the Atlanta executives the most, though no one understood in advance just how clever and quick Pepsi's response would be.

At the same time advertising was being created, William Duncan, the manager of art services at Coca-Cola USA, was furtively trying to assemble promotional materials. He required thirty-eight tons of paper for everything from coupons, point-of-purchase signs, and posters to radio announcements, press kits, and pamphlets for employee communications. And there would be 3,500 bound copies, weighing nine pounds each, of rollout instructions for the bottlers and their employees. "It was by far the biggest undertaking I've ever been involved with— twice the size and complexity of launching diet Coke," said Duncan.

More incredible still, no one in Duncan's art department even knew he was a member of Project Kansas. "You had to do an awful lot of lying," he confessed. "Everybody lied." He made excuses about his hectic schedule, worked nights and weekends, and struggled to keep up with his regular work, just as the other Project Kansas members had to do.

Duncan hired an outside artist with a private studio, a type-setter whose one-man shop was fifty miles outside of Atlanta, and two local printers. Each knew that if the secret leaked out of his firm, he would never work for Coca-Cola again. That loss amounts to a death sentence in the city of Atlanta. To examine proofs of the copy about new Coke Duncan would drive twenty-five miles from Coca-Cola headquarters to meet the typesetter in a bank parking lot in the middle of the night and read the copy by flashlight. At his printer's, a Pinkerton guard was in-stalled, and longtime employees suddenly had to show ID cards to go to work. It so happened that American Graphics was printing a big job order for Lockheed-Georgia at the time, and employees figured that a secret project was behind the veil of secrecy. Once printing for new Coke began, American Graphics screened off part of its plant. The janitors were sent off on a two-week vacation and not a single scrap of paper was thrown away where it could be retrieved by unfriendly hands.

By April, Duncan was frantic. The company, petrified of a leak, told him that he had to be prepared to "do something" overnight should the news escape. That order was easy for them to issue, but Duncan couldn't even get photos of the new Coke can that were to be used in the press kits until the middle of April, a week before the announcement. "I was afraid the last couple of weeks to read the newspaper," said Duncan, "afraid I would see it had leaked, and I was afraid to answer the phone for fear I would hear it had leaked."

On April 1, 1985, Coca-Cola USA presented all the plans and preparations for new Coke to Goizueta, Keough, and a handful of other senior executives. The meeting lasted the entire day. Keough said he found it "tedious" at times, as Dyson again reviewed Coke's decline, the taste-test results, the arguments against a second Coke, and so on. Zyman presented some possible responses from Pepsi, as imagined by the advertising men, and finally he discussed "what could go wrong." He said that consumers, told that new Coke was the elixir of the gods, might expect too much and be disappointed; their backlash in turn would make bottlers edgy and critical of Coca-Cola's decision. But Zyman didn't really believe that this would happen. Nor did Coca-Cola USA, which predicted that any complaints would taper off by mid-May. If some people persisted in their loyalty to old Coke, the company would try to assure them that new Coke was still Coke. And if they refused to be convinced? In the end there wouldn't be a choice, the reasoning being, "Where the hell are they going to go?" No die-hard Coke fan was going to switch camps and drink Pepsi.

They'd far sooner settle for a new taste in Coke than be a traitor to their brand. Such was the confident thinking that endorsed the birth of new Coke.

Although Goizueta and Keough had already voted to change old Coke, although months of intensive work costing millions of dollars had paved the way for new Coke, the chairman at this point could still have said, "No, let's forget the whole risky thing, and get on with business." The meeting adjourned without a definitive, final decision. A night passed. And then, the next morning, Dyson at last got the order he was waiting for: "Go!" Coca-Cola had only twenty-one days in which to tell the bottlers and the board of directors the sensational news, as well as to rehearse for the big press conference at which the momentous change would be announced.

Stout and his assistant, Charles Wallace, had the job of telling nearly all the bottlers. In ten days, they leapfrogged around the country to inform sixty-five bottlers, whose operations accounted for about 90 percent of the volume of sales in the United States. Anticipating that some would contest the decision, Stout had recent research at his fingertips: in taste tests in which he had identified the products as new and old Coke, southerners preferred the former 61 to 39.

For the most part, however, the bottlers didn't need convincing. They liked the new taste. And even in Coke heartland, where loyalty and good business might well have made bottlers intractable, most realized the need for change. Frank Barron, a third-generation Coca-Cola bottler whose territory in Georgia leads the world in per capita sales of Coke, acknowledged, "Sooner or later, what's ailing Coke in one part of the country will creep into another." Not everyone could react with the studied voice of reason, of course, nor with approval. One southern bottler exclaimed, "It was like learning your mother-in-law just drove your Seville off a cliff."

Goizueta, meanwhile, told the radical news to the board members, and the reaction ranged from dismay to skepticism to total support. One member of the board, James B. Williams, was also president of the Trust Company of Georgia, whose vaults guard the secret formula of Coke. A red-haired, freckle-faced good old southern boy, proud of the traditions of the South and of Coca-Cola in particular, Williams had a hard time facing the facts about Coke's decline. Presented with Stout's confidential report, he blanched and then got mad. "I can't believe that," he said. "That can't be right." Goizueta told him that over the past four years the company had undertaken the largest and most expensive research program in its history, and that it all boiled down to one solution: give Coke a new taste. Williams, an ardent admirer of Goizueta and one of his close advisors, eventually agreed. The company had been doing its best to fight against Pepsi, and if Coke just couldn't win, "it had to be taste," he said. He concluded that consumers today wanted either a diet drink or a sweeter one, like Pepsi. Though his instincts were still against a change in Coca-Cola, he gave Goizueta his full backing and confessed, "I'd been faking my-self. I hadn't let myself believe we were getting beaten by Pepsi."

Herb Allen of Columbia, a board member without the southern heritage, offered some prophetic advice. Do Coke Two, but keep number one. When Goizueta explained USA's opposition to this strategy, Allen advised, "Then whatever you do, be ready to do it the other way."

But it seemed that no one really believed in that philosophy. "Everyone was so infatuated with the project that no one would develop contingency plans," Zyman later said. "No one would have listened if someone had said we're going to catch untold hell. New Coke was the greatest thing since sliced bread. It was the diet Coke syndrome—a better-tasting product with the equity of the name Coke. Everybody just said, 'This can't go wrong.'"

The week of April 15, which included an annual shareholders' meeting, the release of the company's first-quarter earnings report, and a mock press conference, culminated in the company's issuing invitations to the nation's media. On Friday, the nineteenth, TV and newspapermen across the country received the following message via news wire and hand-delivered letters:

> Roberto C. Goizueta, chairman of the board and chief executive officer of the Coca-Cola Company, and Donald Keough, president and chief operating officer, invite you to a news conference, which they will conduct on Tuesday, April 23, in New York City, at which time the most significant soft-drink marketing development in the company's nearly 100-year history will be announced.

The importance of the meeting was further emphasized by the company's instructions to journalists in Atlanta, Chicago, Los Angeles, Houston, and Toronto on how to participate via satellite hookup.

That same day, hundreds of calls poured into the Atlanta headquarters. Coca-Cola executives would make no comment, but they had purposely written the invitation in such a way as to send reporters scrambling for an inside scoop. Starting in the Saturday edition of *The Atlanta Journal* and *The Atlanta Constitution*, stories sped across the wires and to the satellites of the Associated Press and United Press International and hit the Sunday editions of many newspapers across the country. Goizueta, who had scarcely slept in three weeks, according to an associate, flew to New York for the day on Sunday to take a final look at the setup at Lincoln Center, where the news conference would be held. By Monday, the national news media, including the *New York Times*, the *Wall Street Journal*, and the *CBS Evening News*, offered full-blown accounts of what Coca-Cola would announce the following day. Still the company would not comment either to confirm or deny the reports.

Pepsi-Cola acted fast. In three short days the company planned and executed an ingenious counterattack, which placed an all-too-revealing spotlight on Coca-Cola and put the world's largest soft-drink maker on the defensive.

CHAPTER 9

THE OTHER GUY JUST BLINKED

The news that burned through the beverage industry on Friday, April 19, left the people at Pepsi-Cola incredulous, though they'd been tracking Coca-Cola especially carefully in anticipation of a change. But what they had predicted was something far less radical, more in keeping with the rumors that had been passed around at regional and state soft-drink-association meetings and at bottlers' conventions—that Coca-Cola might produce a second cola to stand alongside number one.

The president of Pepsi-Cola, Roger Enrico, suspected that the only stumbling block to another Coke was Robert Woodruff, who in 1985 was ninety-five years old, still lucid but nearly blind and deaf. What only Goizueta and a handful of Coca-Cola executives were aware of, however, was that the patriarch had already acquiesced to the idea of a new taste for Coke. When Woodruff died in March, Enrico's comment was "Now they are going to come out with another Coke."

Because Pepsi had had some time to contemplate this possibility, perhaps even plan their retaliation and gauge the effect on the soft-drink market, the news on Friday was all the more astounding. "I was shocked," said Enrico. Others at Pepsi simply couldn't believe that Coca-Cola was going to change its flagship brand.

With only three days to concoct a response, Pepsi-Cola officials snapped into action. Joe McCann, vice-president of public affairs for Pepsi-Cola USA, first tried to predict the key selling point of Coca-Cola's marketing strategy. "My feeling was that they would say that Coke was the greatest soft drink and that now it's better."

Driving home from the Westchester community of Purchase, N.Y., to his apartment in Manhattan, McCann conceived a strategy that would undermine Coca-Cola's pride in its new product and leave it naked and squirming in the public eye. His plan was "to say Coca-Cola is *pulling* their product; not that they are *introducing* a new product; they are pulling Coke off the market and Pepsi's the obvious reason why."

McCann and his wife were giving a party that night, and though by the time he got home the guests had already arrived, McCann went straight to the telephone to call Enrico. The president thought McCann's strategy would work, but he needed time to consider it, because it would represent an abrupt change in company policy.

Since 1983, when Enrico became president, he and McCann had been trying to defuse media publicity about the cola wars. Their feeling was that the two companies' public jabbing at each other, however fascinating to the press, was counterproductive and a senseless expenditure of energy. "Cola wars are interesting to the public because it is a 'war' without victims and a battle without blood and it's easy to choose sides," explained McCann. "But in the end, if we win, what do we win?"

Furthermore, the Pepsi-Cola Company didn't need to denigrate Coke to steal its market. By now Pepsi was so well established and so popular, it could let the facts speak for themselves. For six years it had led in the grocery-store market; the Pepsi Challenge had proclaimed loud and clear which cola tasted better; and the only impediment to Pepsi's becoming number one in the world was Coca-Cola's long-standing contracts with fountain outlets.

For these reasons the young president of Pepsi-Cola had decided to assume a dignified, discreet company stance and maintain a lower personal profile than had John Sculley, his predecessor. In 1983 he withdrew the Pepsi Challenge, which had been airing for eight years. "It had run out of juice," said Enrico, who also agreed with Alan Pottasch, the advertising director, that it was time to return to advertising that focused on image. "Whatever the Pepsi Challenge meant to us, the Pepsi Generation meant more," said Enrico. "Imagery was more important, because over the long haul that's what is going to sustain us, not the Challenge." The centerpiece of Pepsi's image campaign became Michael Jackson, the singing idol. He launched a new slogan, "Pepsi, the choice of a new generation." This seemingly simple phrase in fact cleverly combined the idea of the Pepsi Generation with the Challenge.

Coca-Cola's decision to launch a new cola more similar in taste to Pepsi had to be construed by Pepsi as a direct threat to its own major brand. The company would have to retaliate, and Enrico would have to be the one to direct the counteroffensive.

Just as Coca-Cola's top executives were in the limelight, so he, as president, would have to be Pepsi-Cola's chief spokesman. "It was difficult for him to go out front on this," commented McCann. "But he had to. It was a critical moment in the business." Enrico later quipped, "New Coke got me out of the closet."

On Sunday, April 21, Pottasch and McCann agreed that Pepsi should place full-page ads in the nation's major newspapers on Tuesday, the day of the Coke press conference. On Monday the two officials, along with copywriters from Pepsi's advertising agency, BBDO, convened in Enrico's office to brainstorm. Enrico, meanwhile, was writing the bottlers a letter that turned out to articulate Pepsi's approach better than anything the advertising men could come up with. So with a little fine-tuning, the letter itself became the full-page ad:

> It gives me great pleasure to offer each of you my heartiest congratulations. After 87 years of going at it eyeball to eyeball, the other guy just blinked. Coca-Cola is withdrawing their product from the marketplace, and is reformulating brand Coke to be more like Pepsi. . . . There is no question the long-term market success of Pepsi has forced this move. . . . Maybe they finally realized what most of us have known for years. Pepsi tastes better than Coke.
>
> Well, people in trouble tend to do desperate things . . . and we'll have to keep our eye on them. But for now, I say, victory is sweet, and we have earned a celebration. We're going to declare a holiday on Friday. Enjoy!
>
> Best regards,
>
> Roger Enrico
> President, Chief Executive Officer
> Pepsi-Cola USA

The idea of giving the entire corporation a holiday was brilliant. Such an extraordinary move would be dramatic testimony of Pepsi's confidence. It would also be seen by Goizueta on the very morning of the press conference—"I wanted him to wake up and see that ad in the *New York Times*," said Enrico with relish—and it would startle the press into action. Reporters at the press conference would undoubtedly ask Coca-Cola executives about Pepsi's celebration.

Pepsi-Cola sent a press release declaring victory to most of the media. Its publicity department called two hundred newspaper and magazine reporters to plant the seeds for tough questions to fire at Coca-Cola's top executives. They told the reporters that Coca-Cola was changing the formula because Pepsi was in the lead and that Coke was being made sweeter to taste more like Pepsi. Ask them about those Bill Cosby ads touting Coke's "less-sweet taste," said the Pepsi people. Ask them about the Pepsi Challenge, and whatever you do, don't let Coca-Cola hand you a bill of goods about how "the greatest" has become better—you don't change something that's "so right."

Enrico and McCann were making sure that the right questions would be asked, and that reporters would have all the information they needed to present a solid, serious—even threatening—front. For its part, the press was more than willing to take a lead from Pepsi. Reporters were wary of Coca-Cola's hoopla, the music and banners and patrioteering. They listened well and got ready.

News about a new Coke swept the country on Monday, and the major news outlets weren't about to sit back patiently and wait for the company's confirmation the following day. The

CBS Evening News crew hustled to Purchase, New York, where Enrico was happy to accommodate them, showing them in advance the Pepsi ad that was to run the next morning. The interview aired that night showed the triumphant Pepsi president declaring a company-wide holiday.

Pepsi's final blow to Coca-Cola's grand media event was to hold its own party on Tuesday at noon at Columbus Circle, only six blocks from Lincoln Center. They celebrated with clowns, balloons, banners, and complimentary Pepsis for all the passersby. Many reporters attended the event, and after the press conference some Coca-Cola officials may have come face to face with the festivities.

In three days Pepsi Cola had conceived and organized an impressive retaliation against the king of soft drinks. Coca-Cola, by deliberately baiting the media with the Friday invitation, had forced itself to remain silent for those same three days. They never anticipated that Pepsi could turn the tables so fast. As McCann remarked, "Coke let the news out too early and it backfired, because their hands were tied Monday, and we had all day."

At 7:30 Tuesday morning, Goizueta and Keough attended a technical run-through of the show, to check lights, staging, microphones and video tapes. Everything had been rehearsed, including the carefully orchestrated explanation they would offer for the new formula. What they planned to say would avoid any mention of the real reason for new Coke—the growing success of Pepsi. Because they would not detract from the image and reputation of the world's number one soft drink, Goizueta and Keough could not tell the assembled members of the press that taste tests had again and again showed consumers liked the taste of arch-rival Pepsi better than they liked old Coke. Adrenaline and business savvy would have to carry the two men through this crucial meeting with the press and the many others throughout the rest of the week. They were understandably anxious about what lay before them.

Since they couldn't offer a candid picture, they employed two tactics: They inundated the press with statistics and data, while bragging their way through, joking and sidestepping the questions. In their numerous rehearsals, Goizueta and Keough had tried to anticipate the questions that would be asked, deciding who should address which ones and who would make which jokes. They were extremely well prepared, but they had made a critical misjudgment—the press wasn't nearly as gullible as they had imagined, nor would it be predisposed in their favor.

Shortly before 11:00 A.M. the doors of the Vivian Beaumont Theater at Lincoln Center opened to two hundred newspaper, magazine, and TV reporters. The stage was aglow with red. Three huge screens, each solid red and inscribed with the company logo, rose behind the podium and a table draped in red. The lights were low; the music began. "We are. We will always be. Coca-Cola. All-American history." As the patriotic song filled the theater, slides of Americana flashed on the center screen—families and kids, Eisenhower and JFK, the Grand Canyon and wheat fields, the Beatles and Bruce Springsteen, cowboys, athletes, the Statue of Liberty—and interspersed throughout, old commercials for Coke. No political candidate would have gotten away with such patrioteering without howls of protest, and the members of the press weren't seduced by the hype.

Goizueta came to the podium. Smart and well dressed though

he is, Coca-Cola's chairman is no Ronald Reagan when it comes to addressing crowds and controlling and amusing them with off-the-cuff remarks. He often looks and sounds a bit nervous, with a slight tremor in his voice, perhaps due to the blend of his southern and Cuban accents. This time, at the start, he was wringing his hands. He first congratulated the reporters for their ingenuity in already having reported what he was about to say. And then, as McCann had predicted, he boasted "the best has been made even better."

"Some may choose to call this the boldest single marketing move in the history of the packaged-goods business," said Goizueta. "We simply call it the surest move ever made because the new taste of Coke was shaped by the taste of the consumer."

Sidestepping the years of laboratory research that had gone into the program, Goizueta, claimed that in the process of concocting diet Coke, the company flavor chemists had "discovered" a new formula. And research had shown that consumers preferred this new one to old Coke. Management could then do one of two things: nothing or "buy the world a new Coke." Goizueta announced that the taste-test results made management's decisions "one of the easiest ever made."

With that, the chairman stepped aside and let Keough expound the company's recent successes with diet Coke, Sprite, cherry Coke, and the forthcoming Minute Maid orange soda. He tried to link new Coke with those successes and then, echoing Goizueta, confirmed that the taste-test results were a landslide victory for new Coke. "The best never rest," Keough declared, closing with the statement that he was "darn confident" about the company's decision.

After a preview of commercials that would introduce new Coke, Goizueta and Keough went to sit at a table on the right side of the stage to field the reporters' questions. And now Keough, who was more adept at public appearances than Goizueta, showed signs of nervousness, too, massaging a glass of Coke throughout most of the entire sixty-minute barrage by the press.

Q: "Are you a hundred percent certain that this won't bomb?"

Goizueta: "As I said, it is the surest move ever because the consumers made it."

Keough: "We know we have a winner."

Q: "What's the difference between the new and the old?"

Goizueta: "When you describe flavor, it is a matter better left to the poets or copywriters or members of the press. Why don't you try it and you yourself make the judgment?"

Q: "Put it in your own words."

Goizueta: "I would say that it is smoother, uh, uh, rounder, yet, uh, yet, bolder . . . it has a more harmonious flavor."

(After all the buildup about the great, heavenly taste of new Coke, here was a flavor chemist who couldn't even articulate what it was like. The reporters began to snicker and Keough, in an effort to lighten the situation and empathize with the audience, waved his arms and finally interjected, "You'd make a pretty good copywriter." He wasn't being sarcastic. He just wanted the audience to laugh *with* rather than *at* them, and for the moment he succeeded. Then, more serious, he added, "I think the taste kind of surrounds you.")

Q: "To what extent are you introducing this product to meet the Pepsi Challenge?"

Goizueta: "Oh, gosh, no. That's, uh . . . the Pepsi Challenge? When did that happen?"

Q: "Are you saying that Pepsi-Cola has no more to do with this than Heinz baked beans or Hershey kisses?"

Goizueta: "Well, I don't know. You can certainly handle the English language better than I can, so I'm not going to get into it with you. I can say the consumer had everything to do with it."

Q: "There are those who suggest if it ain't broke, don't fix it."

Goizueta: "While we would agree with you that if it ain't broke, don't fix it, I think an equally important if not more important axiom is that the customer is always right."

Q: "Pepsi in its advertisement today says your change represents an admission that your old product wasn't good enough to make it."

Goizueta (nodding to Keough): "He's a good Irishman, so I'll let him answer that one."

(Goizueta's "Irish" non sequitur was, again, not the best acting technique since it revealed that the two had expected the question and had prepared a reply.)

Keough: "I heard they were taking the day off Friday. You know as an old Irishman we used to celebrate funerals . . . we called them wakes. I'll tell you what, I'd rather be in our position than in that of any other competitor."

Q: "Some people are slow to change. What do you say to those individuals who don't like new Coke and how do you expect to compensate for the market you might lose as a result?"

Goizueta: "Oh, well, we'll just invite them to come and join the party."

Q: "It is true you have lost some market share in the past year or so, so is that a major reason for the change?"

Keough: "The facts are somewhat different than that. In the Nielsen market, in the sugar cola category, it has been a horse race for the last twenty years and Coke has led eleven out of those twenty. . . . The latest bimonthly Nielsen showed our competitor had a point three percent share point lead over Coke in that category, . . . but our overall share in Nielsen grew by over one share point and that represents a big business. And in total market—bottle, can, fountain—we grew our share by over a point in the U.S. and our lead outside the U.S. is expanding dramatically."

Q: "Have you simply added more sweetness to make it more competitive with Pepsi?"

Goizueta: "When it comes to sweetness in soft drinks, it's like when you go to prepare a dessert. You add lemon and then this and then the other thing and then the recipe says add sugar to taste and that's the last thing you come about. . . . Today Royal Crown has the most calories and Pepsi has the next most and then Coca-Cola has the next most, and it will be the same thing tomorrow. . . ."*

* * *

Q: "You say that thirty-nine percent of the people in identified tests preferred the old Coke and forty-five percent in the blind tastes. What does your research tell you of what they intend to do when they are deprived of the Coke they prefer?"

---

* This partial transcript of the conference uses asterisks to mark places where large segments have been deleted to avoid repetition and technical discussion.

Goizueta waved toward Keough, again revealing that the question was anticipated.

Keough: "Well, thirty-nine percent of the people voted for McGovern. . . ."

* * *

Q: "Are you saying that this came about entirely by accident, that your engineers were working on diet Coke and happened to come across this?"

Goizueta: "Not entirely by accident. . . . If they wouldn't have been working that hard, it wouldn't have come about. . . ."

* * *

Q: "Over the last few months you have been running a series of commercials in which Bill Cosby is saying that Coke is less sweet and that's part of its attraction. . . . Now you are offering a soda that is a little sweeter. Are you going to stop running those ads or are you acknowledging that maybe Pepsi was doing something right?"

Goizueta was ready for this one and told Keough to let him handle it: "You would have to agree that those ads were a very good diversionary tactic, don't you? By the way, it is still less sweet . . . or less calories, let me put it that way. . . . Those ads were just to confuse the issue or otherwise we wouldn't have been able to hold this thing as quietly as we did for so long."

* * *

Q: "Did you ever consider marketing both of them, the old and the new under a different name?"

Keough: "No. Basically . . ."

Goizueta (to Keough): Let me say that you and I had discussions and you wanted Keough cola and I wanted Roberto cola and we couldn't get to a middle of the road."

❄ ❄ ❄

Q: "The calorie content: is it the same?"

Goizueta: "All we're talking about is two more calories per twelve-ounce can. . . . You consume twenty-five hundred calories a day and all we're talking about is three more. . . . I can't believe that is the big news of the day. . . ."

(By now Goizueta was visibly annoyed—and confused. If he thought the reporter was asking about the difference in calorie content between new Coke and Pepsi, two calories was correct, but in the same breath he said three. In fact, the question was about new Coke and old Coke. Per twelve-ounce can, the former has ten more calories than the latter.)

Q: "Did you conduct taste tests against the competition?"

Goizueta: "Oh, yes, surely we did, but we don't have to show them. . . . We've had competitors of all colors comparing themselves against Coke . . . but if you're number one, we let others compare. . . ."

Q: "Assuming it's a success, are you planning on reformulating diet Coke?"

Goizueta: "No. And I don't assume that it is a success. It is a success."

Even as the press conference drew to a close, Coca-Cola officials knew it wasn't their finest hour. Why had it gone so wrong?

"We may have given it too much show biz," offered Herbert. Perhaps there was too much hype, and the press, well prepped by Pepsi, viewed it with skepticism if not outright resentment. Furthermore, no intelligent journalist is going to sit quietly and watch his questions being turned into jokes or bypassed altogether. Whenever Goizueta and Keough sidestepped, it merely cued the reporters to heighten the pressure. The press came across as hostile, while the Coca-Cola executives with their tentative answers, "appeared defensive," said Herbert. One of the major pitfalls had come early on, when Goizueta tried to describe the taste of new Coke. Dyson felt that the topic had "not been thought through with enough diligence," and that the company should have been more willing to describe the taste for reporters, who would be passing the product's selling points on to the public. "We should have been more thoughtful, because you're asking people to conjure up their own description," said Dyson. "We weren't talking in consumer-type language." The reporters then had little choice but to pick up on the sweetness and flatness issues, and "that's an unfortunate heritage," remarked Dyson. He also admitted the company didn't do a very good job of explaining why it was introducing a new taste for Coke. "People didn't understand the rationale." How could they, when no one would admit there was anything wrong with the old brand?

Part of the reason for all the hoopla at the press conference was to generate as much publicity as possible, and from that standpoint, anyway, April 23 was an unequivocal success. "I wanted as massive awareness as possible," said Dyson, and he got it. Within forty-eight hours, 80 percent of the U.S. population had heard about the new taste of Coke, according to estimates by outside research firms. And Coca-Cola officials figured that the free publicity during that first week equaled about $100 million in advertising. From there, Coca-Cola pressed ahead with the rollout of new Coke to over two million locations in the United States. If Americans didn't really know why new Coke was coming, they understood very quickly that old Coke was going, that all too abruptly they were losing an old friend.

CHAPTER 10

THE DELUGE

Within forty-eight hours of the press conference, according to several studies, more people knew about the new taste of Coke than knew who was president of the United States. And they weren't shy about their reaction to the smoother, sweeter taste *or* to the company's audacity in making the change.

By early afternoon on Tuesday, April 23, the company's seventeen toll-free hotlines "were flashing like Times Square," according to Roger Nunley, Coca-Cola's manager of consumer affairs. He had watched the press conference, along with 1,500 other Coca-Cola employees, from the Fox Theater in Atlanta. By the time he got back to his "off-campus" office at the Peachtree-Summit building, the calls were pouring in—some 650 in the first four hours.

To handle the anticipated flood of interest, Nunley had up-graded Coca-Cola's toll-free 1-800-GET-COKE lines. This system had begun operating in late 1983, when the number was printed on certain of the company's product packages. By March 1985, seven WATS lines, manned by three employees and a temporary helper, brought in about four hundred calls a day. When Nunley was briefed about Project Kansas, he was told to expect a thousand calls a day—a 150 percent increase— in the first week or two following the announcement. Nunley obviously needed to expand the staff and add more lines to manage the surge in public response. Without disclosing the reason, he asked Coca-Cola employees to volunteer to work two- or four-hour shifts during what promised to be an unusually busy summer. Thirty people applied. On April 19 the walls of three offices were torn down to create additional space for ten new WATS lines and workstations. By Monday, the twenty-second, Nunley had prepared question-and-answer sheets for the telephone operators who would have to explain to consumers why Coca-Cola had a new taste—no easy task, as Chairman Goizueta himself had discovered. On top of that, they would have to assure those consumers that they would like new Coke, offering each caller a coupon for a free six-pack to try it out.

Within five days, the number of daily calls surpassed one thousand and was climbing steadily. Some people were merely curious about how to get the new product, but most were shocked and upset about the loss of a lifetime favorite. This negative consumer response didn't alarm company executives, however, since they had predicted it would take a while for people to digest the news and then sample the superb new product. Furthermore, as Nunley well knew, consumers seldom contact a company with compliments or thanks.

What did irritate Coca-Cola was the national headlines. At the press conference Goizueta had tried to dissuade reporters from harping on calorie count and sweetness as "the big news of the day," but either they hadn't listened well, or they disagreed with his judgment. From coast to coast, on April 24 newspaper headlines highlighted just that feature: "Coke Sweetens the Pop, announced *USA Today;* "The New Coke— A Sweet Swipe at Pepsi," reported the *San Francisco Chronicle.* And, of course, there were accompanying stories with such headlines as "Pepsi Declares 'Sweet' Victory."

Coca-Cola officials continued to deny that either the Pepsi Challenge, or Coke's lost market share, or Pepsi's appeal to the sweet tooth of the youth market had anything to do with the new formula. They kept insisting that Coca-Cola had simply discovered a better-tasting Coke. And while securities analysts did point out that new Coke had been issued to halt the company's market-share slide, they also predicted new Coke would succeed. Why the "harsh reality" of Coke's position wasn't more sharply reported Coca-Cola officials could only surmise. Carlton Curtis, director of corporate communications, felt that beverage industry experts simply "got caught up in the excitement." Perhaps, also, they were leery of blasting Coca-Cola's business acumen, as they had done following the Columbia Pictures acquisition, only to swallow their own words a few months later.

Ironically, by refusing to go public with the harsh reality about Coke, the company set itself up for a more devastating attack. The press wouldn't discuss Coke as a business issue— news that the vast majority of the populace would overlook or readily forget—they would hail the soft drink as an American institution and mourn its loss. They would lambaste new Coke's sweet taste and tearfully recall the old distinctive bite.

The editorial cartoonists especially had a field day. One showed Bill Cosby pouring Pepsi into a can of Coke. Another portrayed the Mona Lisa with punk hairdo and swinging ear bobs, saying, "If Coke can change . . ." The next day, the twenty-fifth, *Newsday's* main headline expressed the trend: "What Have They Done to My Coke?" It was accompanied by a subhead: "The new drink will be smoother, sweeter, and a threat to a way of life."

In Coca-Cola's hometown there was talk of little else. Atlanta has always had a love-hate relationship with its largest company and greatest benefactor. Although residents are proud that the Coca-Cola Company was founded there and are grateful for the revenues it has brought to the city, they also sometimes resent its ubiquitous presence and power. Atlantans were certainly confused when Coca-Cola purchased a motion-picture company, and now they were perplexed about why the company would want to bring a new taste to Coke.

The hometown newspapers, *The Atlanta Journal* and *The Atlanta Constitution*, procured a batch of the new Coke on April 24, even though it wouldn't be in stores in Atlanta for another two weeks. Reporters conducted an informal taste test at the Varsity, the world's largest nonchain dispenser of Coke. The results were overwhelmingly in favor of old Coke, and that information splashed the April 25 edition of the newspaper, along with remarks by the testers. Their opinions echoed conversations held privately all over the city, in kitchens and dining rooms, as natives pondered a change in their way of drinking.

"I don't think Coca-Cola could be improved," said Mrs. Stanley Pitcher. "It's perfect."

"They messed up," Marvin Lites remarked. "You don't change a thing when you got something as good as Coke."

And Lucy Parker delivered the worst possible epithet: "I think you got Pepsi in there with a Coca-Cola label."

Atlanta's reaction sparked correspondents for the *Washington Post*, the *Chicago Tribune* and the *New York Times* to write features revealing that Coca-Cola's hometown was none too happy about the change. Then the columnists and opinion writers jumped into the fray. There were few at the larger newspapers who didn't wax nostalgic and resentful. Michael Kernan, syndicated columnist of the *Washington Post*, remarked bitterly, "Next week, they'll be chiseling Teddy Roosevelt off the side of Mount Rushmore."

Bruce Feirstein, writing for the *Los Angeles Times*, said that the change in Coke was the worst example of the all-too-rapid shift in the American landscape. He mocked Goizueta's explanation that it was altered simply because the company had discovered a better taste: "Now come on, Bob. We all know better than that. The real reason was the Pepsi Challenge."

Jim Fitzgerald of the *Detroit Free Press* lampooned Goizueta's "smoother, rounder, bolder" taste by inferring that old Coke, Fitzgerald's favorite, must have been lumpy, square, and bashful. "I can hardly wait for the announcement that John Wayne was a Communist spy," he quipped.

Bob Greene of the *Chicago Tribune* writes a column that is syndicated in more than two hundred newspapers. He is also the author of eight books, including *American Beat, Good*

Morning, Merry Sunshine, and most recently, *Cheeseburgers.* Greene is a longtime Coke enthusiast. "Every part of my life is associated with Coke," he confessed. Once, while on a layover at Atlanta's Hartsfield International Airport, he took a taxi in to town just to see the Coca-Cola headquarters. It was only a pass around the block, but "it was more moving than visiting the White House," said Greene.

When Coca-Cola made its big announcement, Greene had in fact switched from Coke to diet Coke for calorie reasons, but all his love and nostalgia for his favorite soft drink now were resurrected. He resented the company's attitude, which he described later as "a sort of smugness—that if you don't like new Coke, you will." In late April Greene wrote the first of four columns about Coca-Cola, reminiscing about the Coke he had grown up with, but concluding nobly with a good-luck wish to the company. The column elicited a surprising number of responses—one hundred letters, among them one from Roberto Goizueta "scolding" Greene for "typing when he should have been tasting."

Greene's next column flatly stated that new Coke was a failure. And the last one, written after Coca-Cola decided to return to the old formula, called for the firing of Goizueta and Dyson, whom he characterized as soda jerks.

Greene later commented that his crusade was silly in some ways—"It's just a soft drink." But on the other hand, the unsolicited public response was surprisingly strong; the letters were as vehement and numerous as those he had received some years before when he called for the end of the Vietnam War and the resignation of President Nixon.

The avalanche of stories became so overwhelming that Coca-Cola canceled its clipping service. "Every media outlet throughout the country had a story, and not just once but on several different newscasts and editions," recalled Carlton Curtis. Coca-Cola and its public-relations firm than began compiling clips of articles from only the major newspapers, so that management could keep abreast of the response in those key cities.

Curtis was also collecting what he called "gee-whiz" numbers to use in future presentations to marketing, public-relations, and advertising clubs, which would undoubtedly ask Coca-Cola about how they conceived and launched new Coke. He thought he would have to legitimize his claim that the product was a phenomenon, a huge splash, but "the first week, we realized that no gee-whiz numbers would be necessary," remarked Curtis. "We wouldn't have to convince anyone that this story went off the scale."

Public-relations experts observe that a good news story will be widely reported at first and then taper off. Thus, public-relations executives at Coca-Cola were saying that after the news-weeklies—*Time, Newsweek,* and *Business Week*—had run their stories the week following the press conference, the publicity would begin to subside. That did not happen.

The newsweeklies all carried major stories on new Coke the week of April 29. *Time*'s headline ran "Fiddling with the Real Thing." *Newsweek* declared, "Coke Tampers with Success," while *Business Week* queried, "Is Coke Fixing a Cola That Isn't Broken?" *Business Week* reported that although industry observers were looking for hidden motives for the change, "there don't appear to be any." The article recounted the simple "discovery" of new Coke while the flavor chemists were concocting diet Coke. Even to the business press, then, Goizueta was still acting as if new Coke had suddenly materialized—not that it was the calculated result of years of research, including consumer testing and trial and error in the technical division. And the chairman terminated the discussion by concluding flatly, "I wish the story could be sexier, but it is not."

The sheer volume of responses that first week startled and pleased Coca-Cola. "We were euphoric," said Curtis, "but it was still delicate. We still had to get the product out. We were entering phase two—the rollout."

And roll it out Coke did, covering 90 percent of the country within five weeks, shipping thirty million gallons in May and staging introductory press conferences and sampling parties in forty-five cities. But the celebrated introduction of the new beverage only set the stage for the continuing barrage of negative press stories. Every time Coca-Cola rolled into a new city, it riveted the media's attention, but the stories inevitably quoted loyal Coke consumers who had just tried the new stuff and were quick to voice their displeasure.

When the company was questioned about new Coke's potential, it responded: "It can't fail." And when asked if there was any possibility of bringing back the old Coke, spokesmen unequivocally said, "Never."

The first city to get new Coke was Washington, D.C., part of the Mid-Atlantic Coca-Cola Bottling Company's territory. The company staged a party with a lot of hoopla and free samples for the public. Four blocks from the White House, at Western Plaza, they gave away twenty thousand cans of new Coke in an hour in what the *Washington Post* said was a "mob scene."

In the crowd was John Hayden, a twenty-three-year-old
paralegal who had been drinking Coke since his childhood
days in the Bronx and who now averaged two liters a day.
Hayden was on his lunch hour and he brought back a sample
of new Coke to his office, where he and a co-worker held blind
taste-tests of the old and the new. Both preferred old Coke.

That evening Hayden called his older brother, Thomas, in
New York and told him about the "terrible" taste of new Coke.
Tom panicked and John, in turn, rushed out that very night to
buy the first two of twenty-five cases of old Coke he would
stockpile over the next three weeks.

Hayden not only called Coca-Cola's toll-free consumer hotline, but he also wrote a three-page letter to Chairman Goizueta
and sent twenty copies to the board members and the president
of Mid-Atlantic Coca-Cola. The new taste was terrible, Hayden
wrote, and he accused officials of waiting until after the death
of Robert Woodruff before daring to change the taste of his
Coke.

The people at Pepsi-Cola weren't sitting idle either, of course.
They reminded the public continually that Coca-Cola was de-
nying the most obvious reason for its radical move: the public's
preference for the taste of Pepsi. The reaction to Pepsi's initial
newspaper ad and the subsequent media attention to new Coke
convinced Pepsi executives they could tweak Coca-Cola's nose
with a few more ads that would credit Pepsi with forcing Coca-
Cola's change and at the same time would bolster the Pepsi
system's morale. President Enrico had also ordered that a
brand-new commercial hit the airwaves within a week of Coke's
announcement.

This first spot was called "the letter," although no letter ever appeared. During the weekend of the twenty seventh, Pepsi and its agency, BBDO, tried to film a fifteen-year-old girl writing a letter to the president of Pepsi, asking if he could tell her why Coca-Cola had changed its taste. Six frustratingly unsuccessful hours were spent trying to get the girl to sound and look natural. Finally, on the last take, Alan Pottasch said, "This time, just look into the camera and instead of saying 'Dear Pepsi,' just say, 'Hey, can you tell me why they did it?'"

"It was a one-take wrap," the director of advertising recalled, and it aired on Monday, April 29. In the commercial, the girl is holding a can of Pepsi and after asking if somebody could please tell her why they changed the Real Thing, she takes a sip of Pepsi, emits a sigh of pleasure, and says, "Now I know why."

On May 2, new Coke ventured farther into the South, heartland of its most loyal consumers, with a glitzy party in Birmingham, Alabama. That day's edition of the Birmingham *Post-Herald* carried a story headlined, "Not All Coke Fans Thirsty for New Taste," and it reported the reactions of fifty consumers who were given a sneak-preview sampling of the new taste at one of the city's major malls. It is hard to tell, judging from the quotes, whether these Birmingham residents were more upset at a taste they didn't like or at Coca-Cola for what they perceived as a surrender to Pepsi. To them, it was an extension of the Civil War. Here was Coca-Cola, a southern company, laying down its arms in deference to its Yankee counterpart. Coke, the quintessential southern drink, was changing its image, and content to conform with the rival in the North.

"It seems like they've thrown the towel in, stepped right out of the boxing ring and let Pepsi win," commented Kathryn Cross, who also said she wouldn't patronize restaurants that served Pepsi.

Mrs. E. K. Maxwell told reporter Michelle Berman that she had raised three generations on Coke and she herself had been drinking it for sixty years. "But to concede to competition, I think it cheapens them and makes them look yellow."

At the official May 2 party, Berman asked William Casey, the executive vice-president of Coca-Cola USA, about the original formula.

"We're never going back," stated Casey.

"But what if the new formula doesn't catch on?" persisted Berman.

"I won't even consider it," he avowed.

This conversation, which ran in the Birmingham *Post-Herald*, and other similar declarations from Coca-Cola officials, were like salt in the open wounds of Coke lovers who were left with little hope that the company would reconsider.

Across the continent, far from Birmingham in spirit as well as miles, new Coke arrived at the Los Angeles Coca-Cola Bottling plant. There, according to the *Los Angeles Times*, Brian Dyson hailed the coming of new Coke with strutting bands, red carpet, red banners, red and white balloons, and an airplane towing a banner whose red letters proclaimed "L.A. Loves the New Taste of Coke." When Dyson was asked what would happen if new Coke didn't work, he and the crowd, made up mostly of Coca-Cola employees, merely laughed. "Absolutely impossible," the president of Coca-Cola USA replied.

New Coke was introduced in New York the following Monday, and by Tuesday, Charles Millard sensed "something was wrong." "I was surprised at the number of consumers who were smarter than I was," he said. "Their reaction was so fast and with such clarity that I was concerned from day one." Apparently these consumers knew more about the Coca-Cola Company and its key product than the company itself. They understood that people felt strongly about Coke and that any substitution would be rejected—an insight the crack executive team at the Coca-Cola Company was late to come by.

Two to three weeks later, even though new Coke was selling well in Millard's markets, the bottling company was getting letters and phone calls of protest "way beyond anything before," Millard said. "We were doing pretty good, but the shit was hitting the fan in the South."

Pepsi executives also read newspapers from around the country and they realized that in Coke's backyard, loyal southerners were unhappy with new Coke, even before they tried it. "We realized that the people who were the most upset about the change were those in Coca-Cola's heartland," said Pottasch. That situation provided the germ for another commercial, which aired in mid-May.

Called "Wilbur," the commercial showed three old men, who might have been farmers or retired railroad engineers, sitting on a park bench in a small southern town. Wilbur, the most wrinkled of the three, is pouting, and one of his companions asks him what's the matter. "They changed my Coke," he laments. "I stuck with them through three wars and a couple of dust storms, but this is too much." Wilbur then grumbles that it must have been something big that made Coke change, to which his companion replies, "Right big," and he offers Wilbur a can of Pepsi. Of course, when Wilbur sips the Pepsi, he nods approval.

On May 10, Coca-Cola's hectic rollout reached St. Louis, where Dyson made a revealing faux pas that seemed to underline that the foreign-born executives at Coca-Cola did not fully appreciate how deeply ingrained in American life Coke was. The *St. Louis Post-Dispatch*'s TV critic, Eric Mink, who is also a Coke fanatic, listed for Dyson a litany of American icons, such as the Statue of Liberty, and intimate connections, such as puppy love, that this country associates with Coke. He asked the cola warrior if Coca-Cola was tampering with something as American as baseball, to which Dyson interjected: "Or football?"

A public-relations man accompanying Dyson on the trip was aghast that Dyson had lumped football with America's true pastime, baseball, and he silently gulped and hoped that none of the media would make too much out of this obvious blunder.

Mink later commented that he couldn't believe how narrowly focused Dyson and the other Coca-Cola officials were—on taste —and seemingly unaware of their heretical, "bold" decision.

In Atlanta, Coca-Cola's highest-ranking executives had taken hit after hit from the press, the consumers, and the Pepsi-Cola Company for several weeks following new Coke's debut. With their careers dependent on the success of their bold but "surest" move, they began to worry. As board of directors member Herbert Allen phrased it, "They had bet the crown jewels."

The situation was all the more bewildering because, in contrast to the media response and the burning consumer hotlines,

Roy Stout's weekly survey of nine hundred consumers showed a positive response from the first day. People said they had heard about the change, had tried new Coke, liked it, and would try it again. Shipments are usually a leading indicator of retail sales, and the company's shipment of syrup and concentrate to its bottlers for May 1985 would be up 8 percent over May of the previous year.

Audits & Surveys, Inc., a major independent research firm based in New York that has tracked the consumption of and attitudes about soft drinks for Coca-Cola for many years, also provided some positive data: during May, brand Coke's image surpassed Pepsi's for the first time in years.

The courage of Goizueta and Keough had been demonstrated by their decision to bring out a new Coke. But for that daring move they had tangible marketing data to convince them that something had to be done to keep Coke from disaster. Now they were faced with conflicting evidence on the status of new Coke—the call was very different.

"Don and I started getting these image studies every week from Stout," said Goizueta, "and they showed the image of Coke was going up, but I was traveling, and I would walk into a hotel and they would see my Coca-Cola tag on my briefcase and people would ask me why we had taken away their Coke."

Even the executives' family members expressed dismay over new Coke. In mid-May, Goizueta took a week off from work to attend his son's wedding in Miami. Goizueta's father, who lives in Mexico City, told his son that although new Coke had yet to be introduced south of the U.S. border, Mexico was in an uproar over the pending invasion.

"What have you done?" charged the older Goizueta.

"Have faith in me," the chairman blithely replied.

It was about this time that Keough attended a party at one of Atlanta's most exclusive old-line country clubs, the Piedmont Driving Club. He overheard the following conversation at the bar:

First man: "Have you tried it?"

Second man: "Yes."

First: "Did you like it?"

Second: "Yes, but I'll be damned if I'll let Coca-Cola know that."

Although Keough was aware of the ambiguous relationship between Atlanta and the Coca-Cola Company, and although he had expected resistance to new Coke, the bar conversation indicated that the issue was much larger and more far-reaching than taste alone. It didn't matter how good new Coke tasted; what these people resented was the *audacity* of Coca-Cola in changing the old taste. As Keough explained, the old guard of Atlanta were probably thinking, "There they go again. What do you expect from the guys who put Coke in the movie business?"

Soon afterward came a telephone call that Keough found extremely disturbing. An eighty-year-old woman called the company from California, direct, not toll-free. Though his secretary handled the call, Keough listened in. The woman said she was in a nursing home and for twenty minutes described her fond memories of growing up with Coke. She told the secretary how upset she was that the Coca-Cola Company had taken the product off the market.

It was getting hard for Keough, a man with thirty-five years' experience, to ignore the significance of the individual's reaction, even though standard corporate marketing practices don't usually rely on such anecdotal evidence.

He was distressed, too, by the acerbic calls coming in through the toll-free hotlines. "He was the most affected by the calls because they spoke directly to the heart of the business: image and loyalty," said one of his associates.

In mid-May, Nunley reported that "a surprisingly high number of non–Coke consumers" were jamming the hotlines in protest. The fact that they drank diet Coke or Tab or Sprite or whatever wasn't the point, they said. It was the principle involved. The calls by now were coming in at a rate of five thousand a day, and Nunley's department had to add three more WATS lines for a department total of twenty-two.

In addition to the calls, the postman was arriving daily with pounds and pounds of mail, nearly all of it letters of protest. They spoke of Coke as an American symbol and as a longtime friend that had suddenly betrayed the people. There were critical comparisons of new Coke with Pepsi, threats to switch to tea or water after the stashes of old Coke were gone, and pleas to bring back the old formula. Some of the letters were humorous, some were angry, and many people said that never before had they had sufficient reason to write a letter of complaint. Excerpts from the letters of these irate and opinionated consumers follow:

"Dear Sir: Changing Coke is like God making the grass purple or putting toes on our ears or teeth on our knees."

"It is absolutely TERRIBLE! You should be ashamed to put the Coke label on it. . . . This new stuff tastes worse than Pepsi."

"I don't think I would be more upset if you were to burn the flag in our front yard."

"Monkeying with the receipt is akin to diddling with the U.S. Constitution. . . . Many of us aren't interested in caffeine-free, NutraSweet, diet slop, fancy gimmicks or new formulas. After all these years, the original Coke practically runs through our veins."

"The sorrow I [feel] knowing not only won't I ever enjoy the Real Coke, but my children and grandchildren won't either. . . . I guess my children will have to take my word for it."

"It is too sweet and has no spunk whatsoever. The solution to the problem is simple, return to the original. The worst feeling of all that I get about the new Coke is the feeling that I have been abandoned by a company that has gained my trust and respect for the entire twenty years that I have been alive."

"I can only hope your daring spirit will come forth when you realize the mistake you have made and you can admit it publicly. And that you'll have the guts to go back to the original formula."

"It was nice knowing you. You were a friend for most of my 35 years. Yesterday I had by first taste of the new Coke and to tell the truth, if I would have wanted a Pepsi, I would have ordered a Pepsi not a Coke."

The company did receive letters that praised the taste of new Coke, but they represented a small fraction of the overall torrent of mail. Of course they were savored by the distressed Coca-Cola executives: "Roberto, Brian, and I passed those letters back and forth so often that they are tattered and dog-eared," said Keough.

In all, Nunley's department received and answered more than 40,000 letters that spring and early summer. Each response contained a coupon for a six-pack of new Coke. One woman wrote a second letter, thanking the company for its nice letter, but returning the coupon because she "wasn't about to use it." In addition to the glut of mail, Coca-Cola received 557 petitions signed by 28,138 distraught consumers.

A fear was beginning to take hold at Coca-Cola that this outpouring of rage—based not on displeasure with taste but on the disruption of tradition—might become "institutionalized" and result in permanently disaffected Coca-Cola consumers. "What if they began a boycott of all our products?" was a question beginning to haunt the halls and offices on the top floors at headquarters.

In early May Keough and Goizueta were sufficiently worried to talk privately about the option of returning to old Coke. But they couldn't make a decision to act. They kept saying, "Let's wait and see if this works out," because Dyson and Zyman at USA continued to insist that the protests would subside. Goizueta and Keough kept their doubts to themselves, as if they were sitting on top of a volcano and had to appear resolute to keep the whole system from erupting. "Roberto and I would look knowingly at each other," Keough recalled. By late May, he said, they were like two kids about to open a Christmas gift early.

In New York, Charles Millard was also feeling uncomfortable with the situation, and he discussed with Ed O'Reilly, president of New York Coke, what the results of continued bad publicity might be. Agreeing that a serious problem was developing within just "two to three weeks of the announcement," they raised the issue with Dyson. "Brian was not ready to hear that question," said Millard, "and he looked like he had been punched."

Things went from bad to worse. By Memorial Day weekend, May 25, 26, and 27, a mere four weeks after its unveiling, new Coke was available virtually everywhere in the country. More than a million cans of new Coke had been given away and millions more had been purchased at a discount as the company and bottlers sought as broad exposure as possible. But, also by Memorial Day, the supply of old Coke had evaporated. Consumers no longer had any choice. Their old friend had vanished and been replaced by a stranger, an impersonator. The final disappearance of old Coke from the grocery shelves transformed the tide of complaints into a tidal wave of anger and protests. The forty-five press conferences accompanying the rollout of new Coke had helped to keep the displeasure of loyal Coke drinkers in the news. And they had inspired consumers to call the 1-800-GET-COKE number and pummel the Coca-Cola Company. By the end of May, the consumer affairs department was being deluged with *eight thousand* calls a day.

Right up until this time, Stout's weekly survey still found support for new Coke. In fact, based on interviews with nine hundred consumers (interviews the company had been conducting regularly for ten years), Coke's overall rating had shot way past Pepsi's. For the week of May 27, however, Stout's rating system showed a sudden downturn, signaling a weakening of Coke's image. Worse still, consumers were no longer expressing the intent to repurchase the new formula, as they had indicated earlier.

Still more devastating was the response from kids and teen-agers, a target audience that new Coke was especially formu-lated to attract. During the early weeks of new Coke's intro-duction, the most positive reactions had come from those young consumers. "Seventy percent of the kids said they liked it," Stout said. "But as time went on they were influenced by the adults and became just as negative."

Stout later attributed the May 27 shift to negative press. For example, Paul Harvey, the all-American commentator, declared on his nationally syndicated radio program that new Coke wasn't going to work. He even suggested it would be a coup for the company to bring back old Coke and publicly apologize.

Also about this time, a man was beginning to emerge in the media who would be called the national leader of the Bring-Back-Old-Coke movement. In late May, Gay Mullins was sit-ting in a restaurant in Seattle talking about new Coke with Frank Olson and a few of their acquaintances. They decided to "go after" Coca-Cola, Mullins later said. They thought that if they raised enough of a ruckus, "Coca-Cola might give us fifty thousand dollars to shut up."*

To carry out their plan, Olson and Mullins formed two sepa-rate corporations, the Public Response Corporation and Old Cola of America, Incorporated. According to records in the Office of the Secretary of State of Washington, the "initial

---

* Mullins is the primary source for this account of his protest against Coca-Cola. Olson refused to be interviewed for this book, and, in fact, tried unsuccessfully to dissuade Mullins from telling the story. (He was present briefly during the author's interview with Mullins.) Olson said "their story was worth something."

annual report" filings for both corporations were formally recorded on June 26; however, the date next to Olson's signature
is June 11. Both corporate listings show Olson as president and
treasurer and Mullins as vice-president and secretary. As it
turned out, Mullins became the public spokesman, while Olson
remained very much behind the scenes.

The papers state that the purpose of Old Cola of America
was "to bottle, market and distribute soft drink beverages,"
while the Public Response Corporation's business was "to
monitor new products and product changes in America." What
Old Cola of America actually did is another story. Old Cola
Drinkers of America, as the corporation became known, led a
protest against new Coke and demanded that old Coke be
brought back. Public Response was to become a public-relations
firm of sorts, its founders hoping to get Coca-Cola as a client—
or even Pepsi-Cola. As Mullins himself later admitted, he was
in the business, at least at first, for money, not out of a deep-
rooted loyalty to Coke.

Mullins said that shortly before he had received an $800,000
contract on a building he had sold, and he used that contract
as collateral to borrow money to finance his new efforts. In all,
the loans amounted to about $120,000.. "I had a feeling I would
get it back," he recalled.

The group set up headquarters at the Yesler Hotel in Seattle.
They rented desks and chairs and installed five telephones, including an 800 number, which played a recorded message:
"Let's get Coca-Cola to start making old Coke again." For six
dollars, "protesters" could buy one of the groups' T-shirts,
which pictured a bottle of new Coke inside a circle with a line
through it, symbolizing DON'T.

Mullins's expenses escalated fast. "I paid seven thousand dollars in long-distance calls myself," he said. Attorney fees ate up another $10,000 and travel costs another $25,000. In June Mullins helped stage a rally in San Francisco that cost him $5,000. He even had Coke analyzed for cocaine, spending "thousands"—all for naught. The corporation's earnings, a paltry $1,400, didn't even cover the manufacturing costs of the T-shirts.

But as the protest snowballed, Mullins no longer cared about the money. He became a celebrity, an individual who dared take on a multibillion-dollar corporation. He spoke on about 200 radio shows and appeared in national magazines and on TV shows, sporting his white beard and an anti–new Coke T-shirt.

When *Newsweek* asked Mullins why he was putting so much effort into the Coca-Cola protest, he responded, "Why am I putting my energies into this when people are starving in Ethiopia and dying in Central America? Somebody has to do it. You have to be ever vigilant in our democracy. When they took old Coke off the market, they violated my freedom of choice. It's as basic as the Magna Carta and the Declaration of Independence. We went to war with Japan over that freedom." Mullins went so far as to say that if the company didn't want to bring back old Coke, they should "give the formula to someone else so they can produce the old Coke." He told *Time* he was considering a shot at a seat on the Coca-Cola board of directors.

Across the nation magazines and newspapers were delighted with the colorful champion of old Coke and published his photograph extensively. Millions of Americans saw him mugging for the camera in a tongue-out, thumbs-down pose he poured cans of new Coke into the streets of Seattle.

Despite his fervor, Mullins actually failed to distinguish Coke from Pepsi in tests administered by Erik Lacitis of the *Seattle Times.* In a test of six different cola drinks, Mullins couldn't distinguish new *or* old Coke. In fact he picked Royal Crown as old Coke.

When given only three samples, old Coke, new Coke, and Royal Crown, he again picked Royal Crown as old Coke.

Mullins then was blindfolded and the reporter popped open two cans. Mullins said the new Coke was old Coke, the old Coke, new.

Still, Mullins was enthralled with the fame and glory of the protest. "I had so much goddamn power, as much as Coca-Cola," he later exclaimed. "I was a general leading a campaign . . . and I won. I had a complete feeling, you might say." Mullins said he was "fully functioning" at that time, or "totally utilized." "It was exhilarating, because what stuck in America's mind was that there was one individual who did it and that gives everybody power. We were bigger news than the [TWA] hijacking or Reagan's tax plan."

In Atlanta, meanwhile, the frustration and tension were growing. Some executives still believed in new Coke, still maintained that it ought to work, and rationalized some of the protest movements accordingly: "When they were pouring out the product, we knew it wasn't an evaluation of new Coke but it was a protest over having taken away old Coke," remarked Carlton Curtis. Stout was conducting taste tests, and in blind tests new Coke was still beating Pepsi, but Pepsi was winning overwhelmingly in tests that identified the brands. The very idea of a new Coke was inspiring an extremely negative reaction. "We could have introduced the elixir of the gods," said Ike Herbert, "and it wouldn't have made any difference."

The company was forced to take some unusual steps. Herbert ordered that Coca-Cola's national advertising schedule be cut in half to *reduce* new Coke's visibility for a while. "We were afraid we'd have a nauseous country [if they ran the commercials]," he said. Then Coca-Cola hired a psychologist to monitor the consumer hotline, and he reported that callers were talking as if a member of their family had died.

The sales of new Coke were still looking all right, but Goizueta no longer put much stock in them. "The way people talked and acted was different and you don't have to be a psychologist to know that people start acting like they think." And even if nationwide sales were acceptable, there were places in the South where people were "flat not buying it," said Keough.

The territory served by the Coca-Cola Bottling Company of Rome, Georgia, contains some of the most fervid Coke fans in the world. When those consumers rebelled, when store owners couldn't move new Coke and wanted to return it to the bottler, the Coca-Cola Company couldn't look the other way. Frank Barron, principal owner of that bottling company, had started out an enthusiastic supporter of the new product and had gotten it onto the shelves quickly and efficiently. But consumer retaliation was equally efficient. "The cults began asking us if we had any of the old Coke we would sell them, and they were disrupting the shelves looking for the old," Barron said.

By the end of May, Barron and many other southern bottlers

were very upset. The marketing committee of the Coca-Cola bottlers' association held a meeting in Atlanta, and members were shown the results of Stout's weekly monitoring of public opinion. People liked new Coke better than old Coke by two to three percentage points, claimed Stout.

"Shouldn't it be more like seventy to thirty or eighty to twenty?" demanded Barron. "Two or three points doesn't seem like a lot." The cheerful researchers told the bottler that the problem was he didn't understand statistics.

To the bottlers, to the employees, and to the consumers, Coca-Cola was straining to appear united in its allegiance to new Coke, trying to seal any cracks through which rumors of unrest or further change might escape. People at Coca-Cola who surmised that new Coke wouldn't survive, or at least wouldn't survive alone, kept their thoughts closely guarded.

The situation at the end of May was dire enough so that Dyson, new Coke's champion, was finally discussing some options with Zyman. They could do more sampling of the product, convinced as they were that it was a superior cola, or they could conduct a Coke Challenge against Pepsi. Keough opposed the idea of "the leader" stooping to comparative advertising. Zyman even discussed the possibility of "transferring the equity of Coke to cherry Coke," by which he meant taking cherry Coke, which was doing extremely well in test markets, and rolling it out nationally and trying to persuade consumers that this was old Coke but with a little cherry in it. It is not likely that option was ever seriously considered. Dyson and Zyman did consider the idea of bringing back old Coke, but once again they opted simply to wait. "We were saying it would die down," Zyman recalled. "We kept saying, it doesn't look like a winner but we've got to make it one."

Goizueta and Keough, on the other hand, had pretty much made up their minds by early June how to address their situation. "What the hell, let's do it"—bring back old Coke—agreed the weary and worried top executives. The tactical problem was that new Coke was really in USA's charge—under the leadership of Dyson and Zyman. Goizueta and Keough didn't want to interfere too quickly, nor did they want to undermine the position of Dyson, a powerful man whom they esteemed. The result was that even after Keough and Goizueta were fairly certain the change had to be made, Keough decided to ride a bit further on the president of USA's instincts.

CHAPTER 11

THE SECOND COMING

By June the anger and resentment of the public was disrupting the personal lives of Coca-Cola employees, from the top executives to the company secretaries. Friends and acquaintances were quick to attack, and once-proud employees now shrank from displaying to the world any association with the Coca-Cola Company. "Some of the top officers weren't invited to parties," said Ike Herbert. At one of his own parties "a used-to-be friend became very hostile" toward him over the Coke issue, and his tennis partner "let him have it constantly."

In June, Frank Barron went through customs in Vancouver, and when the agent discovered his occupation, she took five minutes to speak her mind about Coke. "You guys really messed up," she charged, and proceeded to "give me hell," said Barron. The wealthy bottler belongs to one of the leading families in Rome, Georgia, and like other Coca-Cola executives, he found that increasingly he was "catching hell at parties." He finally gave up going to his country club and told his wife he was going to become a recluse. Even from shopkeepers and grocers Barron tried to conceal his identity. For years he had placed his Coca-Cola business card with its embossed red logo in his wallet so that when he opened it to pay for purchases, it would identify him. But now, this third-generation Coca-Cola man had to turn his card facedown to avoid confrontations. The bottlers' route salesmen and delivery men were under continual fire too. "My delivery men were the most devastated men I've ever seen," said Barron. "A few even threatened to quit."

What, in fact, did all this anger mean for new Coke? By mid-June, "our Coke volume had gone to hell in a handbasket," remarked Barron about sales in his area. This was, of course, a critical factor for Goizueta, who had suspected that the complaints would soon translate into declining numbers. "Sooner or later they may stop buying," worried the chairman. "I can put up with flak with sales up, flak doesn't bother me, but I can't when sales are down." Although May sales had been quite good, he anxiously awaited the numbers for June.

He was waiting, too, for Brian Dyson, the champion of new Coke. Coca-Cola USA was still advocating that the company endure the furor until the end of the year, by which time it would surely burn out. Until that vital part of the company had a change of heart, Goizueta simply did his best to restore equilibrium, both inside and outside the company. To boost employee morale, he and Keough led a pep rally on June 10 at the Fox Theater in Atlanta, where they promised all nonmanagement employees a special $100 summer bonus.

Goizueta was attentive to the investment community, too. On June 11 he and Keough, Doug Ivester (now chief financial officer), and some major bottlers met with securities analysts to assure them that Coca-Cola would do whatever was necessary to maintain its dominance of the soft-drink industry. It was one of thirteen meetings the company held between April and November with various analysts and institutional investors, representing four hundred different investment institutions. These meetings, and the confidence the investment world maintained in the management of the Coca-Cola Company, account for the paradoxical steadiness of Coca-Cola's stock during that summer when consumers were outraged.

On June 15, Goizueta and Keough flew to Monte Carlo for a week-long conference with the largest bottlers in the world. The top Coca-Cola officials appeared collected and controlled, never hinting to anyone the slightest intention of bringing back old Coke. Charles Millard announced that his territory "was settling down," and that they "could stay the course." Millard felt Goizueta and Keough were masking deep anxiety about the prospects for new Coke. "I got the definite sense that New York was atypical," he commented, "and that they were considering bringing back the old product."

On their last night in Monte Carlo, Mr. and Mrs. Goizueta and Mr. and Mrs. Keough dined at a very small, intimate restaurant outside town. Wishing to pay his respects to the eminent Coca-Cola officials, the owner brought to their table a six-and-a-half-ounce bottle of Coke, chilled, in a wine bucket. "This," he said proudly, "is the old Coke."

Keough and Goizueta rose to the occasion and remained composed, but the scene epitomized the world's feeling about old Coke. Here was a country that didn't even have new Coke yet, but the negative message had already crossed the ocean.

Brian Dyson didn't go to Monte Carlo because he was determined—"come hell or high water"—to attend the elaborate one hundredth-anniversary celebration of his family's 4,400-acre ranch in Argentina. With his wife and two daughters, Dyson left Atlanta on June 18, arrived in Buenos Aires on the nineteenth, and finally reached the ranch on the twentieth. By the following day, Coca-Cola had caught up with him. Frank Morley, his executive assistant, called the Coca-Cola office in Buenos Aires on Friday the twenty-first, as Dyson had requested, to relay the results of Stout's June 19 weekly survey of new Coke. Since the ranch had no phone, a Coca-Cola employee then drove five hours to the ranch and delivered a taped recording of Morley's message. The president of Coca-Cola USA was planning to spend nearly two weeks in Argentina, but once he got the update, he told his family he was cutting the trip short. "It wasn't a dire message or anything of the sort, but it was a continuation, just one more week of bad results," said Dyson. "Something clicked that said I can't afford to be away."

Back in Atlanta, Dyson's right-hand man, Sergio Zyman, was getting only about three hours' sleep a night during the long, hot summer of new Coke. The slim Mexican lost ten pounds as he worked seven days a week trying to hold things together. The consumer hotline, for example, was a special interest of his, though the decision to increase the WATS lines had been hotly contested. Roy Stout felt that promoting the 800 number only aggravated the situation and encouraged consumers to call. Zyman held that if there were complaints, "Let's manage them."

Coca-Cola hired college students on summer break to augment Nunley's consumer-affairs department. The offices became known as "the blob" as they spread throughout the Peachtree-Summit building to accommodate 69 college students, 27 agency temporaries, 12 company retirees, 30 freelancers, and 20 permanent members of the staff. A total of 158 workers were now operating 83 WATS lines.

Zyman not only monitored the 800 number, he called it a few times himself. "The biggest problem with the 800 number," he said, "was that some of the operators were also pissed off" and obviously couldn't address the issue of the superiority of new Coke very convincingly. Some of the consumers he listened to talked as if Coca-Cola had just killed God, said Zyman, adding, "You can't reassure people about killing God." The calls, more than anything else, brought home to Zyman the country's depth of feeling for Coke.

On June 21, Carlton Curtis visited the consumer hotline offices for the first time. He listened in on a call from a woman from Mississippi, who sounded mature and intelligent. But when the young college student in the company office described the taste tests that had been conducted and how many people preferred the new taste, she cut him off short: "Young man, I hate coffee, but I drink it all day long." In other words, the woman didn't care how good new Coke tasted—that wasn't the point. She was upset because she wanted *her* drink, the old Coke.

The national press was underscoring the same message. The week of June 17, *Time, Newsweek*, and *Business Week* again carried stories on growing protest movements against new Coke. *Newsweek*, in its national affairs section, announced, "saying 'No' to New Coke: Diehard fans of America's favorite soft drink mount a nationwide campaign to bring the old stuff back." *Time* reported, "All Afizz over the New Coke. Some hate the taste, but sales have never been better."

Though they told no one about it, by mid-June the company had secretly increased the acidity level in new Coke in an attempt to correct the flatness that consumers were complaining about. Zyman later revealed that he had even made a "demo" commercial explaining that the company had "put the bite back." But the commercial never aired and the company never announced any such change. To this day, executives deal only indirectly with it. "There might have been some tinkering with phosphoric acid levels" as well as with the carbonation levels, they acknowledge, but that change was simply to keep new Coke, then being produced in huge volumes, uniform with the prototype. Curtis admits that "the early product might well have been different," but he insists that merely correcting the acidity and carbonation levels didn't constitute a formula change. The essential oils, "the real essence," remained the same, officials still maintain.

When Millard returned from Monte Carlo to his New York office on June 22, "The place was like a morgue." Business and morale were down; the mail and the telephone calls were escalating. Millard and O'Reilly decided that New York Coke needed its own consumer research on this growing menace. From the one thousand people who had written or called to complain, three hundred were chosen to be interviewed by telephone. Another three hundred New Yorkers, who hadn't called or written, were selected at random. Oddly enough, it was this group of nonprotesters that frightened Millard the most. "They were as angry as the other group—that was the scary part," confided Millard. "There were people who said they had tried it three times—had tried to like it—but they didn't."

When Marvin Griffin, chief executive officer of the Consolidated Coca-Cola Bottling Company, returned from Monte Carlo to his offices in Charlotte, North Carolina, his marketing department told him, "The world has turned to shit." Sales were not going at all well, and employees were beginning to doubt new Coke. But Griffin countered, "The saying 'If it ain't broke, don't fix it' is a motto for losers." If the company operated under that motto, he said, there would have been no diet Coke, no new Tab (with NutraSweet), and Sprite would not have been improved to become a close second to 7-Up. Griffin told his employees the real change had taken place a long time ago, the day Coca-Cola decided to use packages other than the six-and-a-half-ounce bottle.

Larry Smith, the champion of the Pepsi Challenge, had defected to Coca-Cola in 1983 and was now head of the Miami Coca-Cola Bottling Company. He too encountered employees who were beginning to believe all the negative press and who "weren't following through" at the retail level. "They believed old Coke was better," said Smith. He reminded them about the Pepsi Challenge, the reason that new Coke had been introduced in the first place, and how they themselves had convinced the retailers and chain stores that Coke was better.

"We had to go show them that they didn't have to be afraid of chain stores," said Smith, who remained a new Coke enthusiast, while other southern bottlers "were screaming."

"Texas became a disaster area," said Ike Herbert. At a regional meeting held in Dallas in mid-June, the bottlers signed a petition asking the company to bring back old Coke. The bottlers were unaccustomed to public criticism. They didn't like it mainly because it undermined their pride in their own product. Rather than supporting new Coke, they agreed with the critics that old Coke was better. "After the new-Coke flak started, the southern bottlers went to their country clubs and forgot about the Pepsi Challenge," said Goizueta.

Dyson returned to Atlanta on June 27 to be told by Keough that if old Coke was withheld much longer, there could be permanent damage to the goodwill the company had enjoyed for so long. Stout's survey results were continuing to show Coke's image "tracking downward" against Pepsi's, and more people than not were saying they preferred old Coke to new Coke. Preliminary reports were showing that June sales of new Coke would be weak—weaker than had been hoped, and only about equal to the sales of old Coke the previous June.

Keough paid little attention to sales, however. "My own view is that sales volume had nothing to do with it," he explained. "There were pockets of problems, particularly in the South, but the public outcry was too big, too constant, and too real."

Dyson told Keough that by July 8, Coca-Cola USA would recommend one of three courses of action: persist with new Coke, or wait just one more month to see what happened, or bring back old Coke. Although Dyson was still inclined to believe that things would improve, Zyman was now nudging him too. He advocated bringing back the old formula under the name Coca-Cola original. "The whole thing is about to come to an end," said Zyman, "and once it dies, you could lose half your market share. The people who are upset could stay upset and the others could quit caring. It's about to die and you don't know which way it'll go."

By the first of July most of the bottlers were reading local June numbers that were similar to those received at headquarters. Many began demanding that old Coke be brought back, although bottlers in Miami, Los Angeles, and Detroit stood fast by new Coke. On July 3, Millard and O'Reilly from New York, Griffin from Charlotte, and several other large bottlers met with Dyson. "We have got to come back with old Coke," asserted Griffin. "America is saying, 'You've taken away my Coke.'"

He sensed that personal pride was blinding Dyson and his USA team to the facts before them. After all, it was only two years after such grand successes as diet Coke, the franchise restructuring, and the rejuvenation of Sprite. This was a group of executives used to making sharp decisions and enjoying the subsequent success. It was hard for them to accept failure, especially on a project on which four million dollars had been spent. Yet here were Griffin and several other major bottlers, who had fully supported new Coke at the outset, saying less than three months later that the product was a failure. "Dyson didn't want to hear it," commented Millard, "but Brian is a good listener."

On Friday, July 5, Dyson held a major meeting of his USA team to discuss the latest information available and gauge the group's opinions about what to do. At last USA reached a consensus to bring back old Coke, but Dyson himself, new Coke's tireless defender, was still casting about for another acceptable, rational course of action. He told the group he wanted the weekend to think it over.

By now Keough felt certain that Dyson would concede but even before he did, Keough, on July 5, set in motion the corporate, public-relations, and financial departments to prepare for the reintroduction of America's old favorite. That same evening the *MacNeil-Lehrer Newshour*, a prime-time TV news program, devoted twenty minutes to the Coca-Cola phenomenon and showed a lot of angry consumers pouring new Coke out onto the streets.

On Sunday, July 7, Carlton Curtis, corporate communications director, together with Earl Leonard and Garth Hamby, flew to New York. At the International Hotel they met with Harold Burson of Burson Marsteller, one of the world's largest public-relations firms. The men sat around a table "with a clean sheet of paper," said Curtis, and worked as if the decision to bring back old Coke had already been made. "We didn't know when we would make the announcement, but we knew it wouldn't be weeks," he recalled. One person wrote the speeches, one wrote the press release, and another wrote the question-and-answer crib sheet. "It was relatively simple and uncomplicated," remarked Curtis. "The message was: We've heard you." Like the company, Curtis's group maintained that the public's reaction wasn't "a slap at new Coke but at the decision to withdraw old Coke."

On the following day, July 8, Dyson met with the board of governors of the Coca-Cola Bottlers Association. "Brian gave an absolutely brilliant and objective review of the situation," commented Millard, "and knowing where his heart was, if not his head, that was admirable. I think he came to that meeting with an open mind but hoping he wouldn't have to recommend bringing back old Coke." Although no formal vote was taken, Dyson understood the consensus of the bottlers: Bring back old Coke—and fast. "He left the meeting with his heart where his head had been," said Millard.

Late that afternoon Dyson reported to Keough that he finally concurred with those who favored bringing back old Coke.

For some weeks—even before the final decision to reissue old Coke—company officials had been arguing about what to call the drink if it was introduced. Goizueta was growing increasingly impatient over the long, painful ordeal. "It took the month of June to get USA to decide to bring back old Coke," he complained. "It took two weeks to name it." Goizueta and Keough wanted to call it "Classic," but Coca-Cola USA stood behind "Original." "Sergio and Brian were saying that no one would understand what 'classic' meant," Goizueta said. Clearly irritated, he added, "The same people who wanted 'original' were the ones saying hold out until the end of the year."

On July 9, the chairman called a meeting on the twenty-fifth floor of the Tower to put an end to the ongoing debate. There, Goizueta, Keough, Herbert, Dyson, and general counsel Robert Keller discussed the two options: "classic" versus "original." Keller pointed out that in the bottlers' contracts "original" is used to refer to Coca-Cola. That product was now new Coke; therefore, the company could not market another product with that name. Also, according to the contracts, the bottlers had to take Coca-Cola; since several did not even want old Coke, a "classic" Coke could be optional.

"I told Brian the arguing is over; it's 'Classic,'" asserted Goizueta. "Brian said I let the lawyers name the product."

At the meeting the Coca-Cola executives also decided to hold a press conference on Thursday, July 11, to announce their decision. But on July 10, rumors began circulating that old Coke was returning. Peter Jennings of ABC News interrupted the daytime soap opera *General Hospital* to report that old Coke was returning. The company was then forced, through fear of violating securities laws, to release a short statement Wednesday afternoon verifying that old Coke would soon be back.

As word began to spread, the hotline telephones rang as never before. On July tenth alone, the company received twelve thousand calls. Within Coca-Cola the heralded event was called the Second Coming.

Keough, meanwhile, was busy taping his first major television commercial, which had to be beamed via satellite to New York in time to make the major network newscasts that evening. ABC and NBC led with the news of the return of old Coke; CBS made the announcement about a third of the way through its nightly news. Even ABC's prestigious *Nightline* devoted thirty minutes to Coca-Cola's welcome news that Wednesday night.

On Thursday virtually every major newspaper in the country carried a front-page story about old Coke's return. And although the news was already widespread, reporters flocked to the press conference that morning. Some 150 newsmen crowded into the auditorium of Coca-Cola USA, but the scene was entirely different from the press conference just three months before. Here, there was only one satellite feed, which went to New York. There was no fancy show and no audiovisual extravaganza. The press conference was called so quickly that the copies of Dyson's remarks distributed to the press contained blacked-out phrases and handwritten insertions. Frank Barron later said he was afraid that when Classic was brought back "they would be arrogant about it." But this time there was none of the cockiness that the top executives had demonstrated in April. "We tried to be as humble as possible," said Goizueta.

Goizueta, Keough, and Dyson walked onto the stage in front of the Coca-Cola logo to make an apology to the public—without admitting that new Coke had been a total mistake, however. "Today, we have two messages to deliver to the American consumer," said the chairman. "First, to those of you who are drinking Coca-Cola with its great new taste, our thanks. . . . But there is a second group of consumers to whom we want to speak today and our message to this group is simple: We have heard you."

Goizueta went on to talk about taste-testing as he had not done before: "Since the announcement [of new Coke], in countless blind taste-tests, the majority of the soft-drink-consuming public has consistently told us they prefer the new taste of Coke over Pepsi. However, I would be less than candid if I did not tell you that not all consumers felt that way. To them, nothing could compare with the unique taste of the original formula for Coca-Cola. To them, original Coca-Cola was indeed a classic."

Goizueta told the group that the Coca-Cola Company had attained the position it enjoys by watching consumers, listening to consumers, and giving them what they want. Although assuming unprecedented humility, he could not refrain from adding: "After everything is said and written about Coke and Coca-Cola Classic, two clear facts remain. Firstly, never before in its history has this Coca-Cola system been stronger or better equipped to do its job. Secondly, despite claims of one kind or another, sour-grape comments or paid ads in newspapers by some of our competitors, not a single one of them can match or will be able to match the sales and share of Coca-Cola and its supporting cast of brands."

Dyson attributed the entire public outcry over Coke to the fact that "a new soft-drink market segment has emerged." He made it clear that new Coke would continue to be the company's flagship, premier brand and would "satisfy more needs and more consumers than ever before."

Dyson boldly predicted that with new Coke, Coke Classic, and cherry Coke on the market, more than half of the colas consumed in America would bear the trademark Coca-Cola by the end of 1985. Furthermore, since the trademark also appears on diet Coke and the caffeine-free versions of Coke and diet Coke, one out of every three soft drinks of any kind consumed in the United States would carry the trademark Coca-Cola by the end of 1985.

But this conference truly belonged to Keough, the toastmaster general, and he seemed to relish bowing modestly and owning up to an error. "Do we wish that every regular Coca-Cola drinker had fallen in love with the new taste of Coke? Of course we do. Are we totally pleased with the results as we stand here on July 11? Of course not."

After expressing his confidence in new Coke and the company's commitment to there being "only one worldwide Coca-Cola," Keough asked, "What on earth brought us to the decision to bring back the classic taste which we so calmly abandoned back in April? There is a twist to this story which will please every humanist and will probably have the Harvard professors puzzling for years.

"The simple fact is that all the time and money and skill poured into consumer research on the new Coca-Cola could not measure or reveal the deep and abiding emotional attachment to original Coca-Cola felt by so many people . . . the passion for original Coca-Cola—and that is the word for it: passion— was something that caught us by surprise. . . . It is a wonderful American mystery, a lovely American enigma, and you cannot measure it any more than you can measure love, pride or patriotism.

"There is only one kind of primitive measure you can take: You can answer your phones and read your mail, and did we answer our phones and read our mail!" Keough then jokingly thanked the members of the press for "keeping us so happily informed" about the public's outcry over new Coke.

Then, in a self-deprecating move that the audience ate up, Coca-Cola's president read a few excerpts from some of the more humorous negative letters the company had received. He apologized to the thousands of callers and letter writers. "We want them to know we are sorry for any discontent we may have caused them for almost three months."

Keough even thanked Gay Mullins for his efforts, although he did point out that Mullins had picked new Coke over old Coke in blind taste-tests.

People were saying the return of old Coke was a company retreat and a victory of the public over a corporation, said Keough. But instead of disagreeing, he exclaimed, "How I love that! We love any retreat which has us rushing toward our best customers with the product they love most. We love any victory of the public which proves so conclusively that this company does listen, does read its mail, does care with all its heart for all of its consumers. Our boss is the consumer.

"Some critics will say Coca-Cola made a marketing mistake. Some cynics will say that we planned the whole thing. The truth is we are not that dumb and we are not that smart."

During the brief question-and-answer period, Keough confessed that the last three months "had been a humbling experience." Goizueta said, "It's nice to be loved again."

He was referring to the outpouring of thanks the company's hotline was receiving. That day, the consumer affairs department recorded *eighteen thousand calls*. One caller said she had just found out she was pregnant and didn't know which her husband would be happier about—their first child or old Coke's return.

"You would have thought we had invented a cure for cancer," Herbert said.

EPILOGUE

The day after the formal announcement of Classic's return, Keough was sitting in his office with a reporter and Carlton Curtis when his secretary buzzed and said that Gay Mullins was on the telephone. Keough took the call.

Ever the salesman, Keough graciously thanked Mullins for "being so persistent about it. We came to the conclusion that you were right." Mullins told Keough he had been a good warrior and Keough signed off by saying, "You won."

Keough then instructed Curtis to see if there was any way that Coca-Cola might use Mullins in promoting Classic. Someone representing Mullins had already approached Coca-Cola USA, before Classic's return, about working out some sort of arrangement, and Coca-Cola was "considering it." Pepsi, on the other hand, had turned Frank Olson down when he had called Ken Ross and identified himself as "Mullins's boss."

After Classic's return, Curtis said, Coca-Cola "looked closely

at using Mullins as an ambassador for Classic." The Public
Response Corporation submitted a formal proposal in late July,
calling for a $200,000 fee, plus $1,000 and expenses for each
appearance Mullins would make on behalf of Coke. There was
a separate proposal for the consulting work Public Response
Corporation would do, but the dollar amount was not
mentioned.

While the proposal was before Coca-Cola, the Sugar Association launched a short-lived attack on Classic, claiming that it
was not "the real thing" at all because it was sweetened with
high-fructose corn syrup, whereas the original Coke contained
sugar. In fact, since 1980 the company had allowed its bottlers
to use high-fructose corn syrup, which is less expensive than
beet or cane sugar. Coca-Cola maintained, under a technically
correct premise, that high-fructose corn syrup is sugar, and that
sugar is sugar.

After the Sugar Association placed an adversarial advertisement denouncing Classic in thirteen newspapers, Mullins told
Time magazine, "Corn syrup is like lead in my stomach. It
doesn't give me the lift. It makes me sleepy."

Mullins had seized this opportunity to play his tune, he later
said, because "we were interested in being supported by the
Sugar Association." He went on to describe how his group had
been planning a "pour-in," whereby every twenty-four hours
"we would pour out a bottle of Classic because it didn't contain
sugar. We didn't do it because the Sugar Association didn't
fund us."

Neither did Coca-Cola after he denounced high-fructose corn
syrup.

By then, however, the company didn't need Mullins. It was

clear that the public's response to Classic was overwhelming and positive and that it would continue to be so. After the grateful phone calls came letters, hundreds of them, thanking the company for listening to consumers and bringing back their old friend. Letters continued to arrive as late as November. One mother wrote to say "Coke" was her baby son's first word. "Then he said 'more Coke.'" All told, the consumer affairs department estimated it had 400,000 contacts with the public.

As the southern summer waned outside of Coca-Cola headquarters, a sort of peace returned inside. Now that the furor was over, it was time to try to understand what had happened over the last month and what the implications were for the company.

Certainly, to an outsider, it would seem that if the return of Classic so soon after its withdrawal showed anything, it was the flexibility of Coca-Cola's management. That willingness to change allowed the company to admit it had been a mistake to take old Coke off the market. But though the company brought it back, executives stopped short of admitting that new Coke had been a mistake—even as end-of-the-year numbers showed Classic outselling new Coke eight to one or better in many markets.

Dyson predicted that eventually new Coke would take the lead: "Although the consumer consecrated old Coke, if ten years down the road Classic is still the best-seller, it would be unique to marketing. You need tastes of tomorrow and you need to be free to update and keep on the leading edge. . . . New Coke is going to be the standard for the future."

Goizueta and his colleagues had tried to be as humble as

possible at the July 11 press conference, but by late fall the chairman was saying, "I think we were humble a little too long." He was referring to Keough, who characterized the episode as "out of a Frank Capra movie," where the little guy wins. Keough knew a good story when he heard one, and during several speeches he referred to Coke's "humbling experience." Goizueta finally told him that the time for apologizing was over.

In November 1985, discussing what had happened, Goizueta said, "With imperfect forecasts, your strategy has to be flexible." He went on to list three scenarios that the company could have encountered:

First, "Announce new Coke and get yawns," which to the chairman would have been the worst-case scenario. "Imagine all the promotions we would have had to make to get the kind of awareness we got."

Second, "Make a perfect forecast of what actually happened: all the protests and the letters, etc. If we had made a perfect forecast, we would still have announced new Coke, but we would have brought out Classic on May 15."

Third, "Make an imperfect forecast, which happened. We knew we were going to have disgruntled customers, but we didn't know there would be that many. We would still be in the same position today [early November]."

In postmortems across the country the question asked was: Did it all happen because Dyson and Zyman, and even Goizueta, are not native Americans? Perhaps they simply didn't appreciate the depth of the feelings that Americans had about Coke; perhaps they didn't understand that Coke was too much of an American institution to be tampered with.

If this was so, where, then, was Keough, the all-American boy from the Midwest? Keough bristled at the suggestion that he should have known better and prevented the uprising. "The idea of a Latin mafia that conspires without the input of the president is sheer crap," Keough said. He claimed that Goizueta and Dyson understand the American psyche as well as he does. (He omitted crediting Zyman with the same understanding.)

In fact, Dyson and Zyman had pushed new Coke but Herbert, Stout, and other American-born marketers within the company also cheered new Coke along. The bottlers, as in touch with the American psyche as anyone, were in near unanimous agreement with the decision to tamper with Coke. The "foreign element" explanation does not seem to work.

In the months to come, in the wake of the decision to sell both new Coke and Coke Classic, the company's marketing strategy would shift emphasis from specific brands to categories —in this case, the sugar-cola beverage category, including new Coke, Classic, and cherry Coke. Next, the "megabrand strategy" was developed. All drinks with the name Coke were included— Coke, Coke Classic, cherry Coke, diet Coke, caffeine-free Coke, caffeine-free diet Coke, and, by 1986, diet cherry Coke.

What did this brand grouping accomplish? The company's share and volume of the sugar-cola category *did* increase, but that was owing to cherry Coke, not Coke or Classic, or even those two combined. As to the megabrand approach, it provided a new way of reading numbers. Whereas the concern in the past had been that Pepsi-Cola might become the number-one brand, Coca-Cola now said that was "no big deal." It was the *total* sales that counted.

"So what?" Goizueta said of Pepsi's strength. "Mondale can say he won D.C. and Minnesota. Big deal. We outsell our nearest competitor in the six-and-a-half-ounce bottle fifty-to-one. So what?"

By the end of 1985, no matter which industry expert's numbers you chose, Pepsi-Cola had become the number-one brand in the land. The year-end soft-drink report issued by John C. Maxwell, Jr., is considered one of the most authoritative sources for the industry. An analyst with the New York–based brokerage firm Furman, Selz, Mager, Dietz & Birney, Maxwell shows in his 1985 report that neither the combined volume nor market shares of new Coke and Classic reached the level of old Coke's 1984 performance, though they came close. At Coca-Cola's request, Maxwell lumped together the figures for old Coke prior to April 23 and new Coke thereafter. Classic was given credit only for its volume and share after July 11. Using this method, which obviously makes new Coke's performance look better than it really was, the survey rates Coke with a 14.1 percent total market share and Classic a 7.1 percent market share. However, if you glance down at the footnotes that explain the method, you could virtually reverse those numbers.

Almost unnoticed in the numbers game was cherry Coke, which, according to Maxwell, had an even more successful introduction than diet Coke. In national distribution since August 1985, the cherry-flavored version of old Coke had achieved number-ten or number-eleven rank.

As for Pepsi, Maxwell ranks it number one and gives it a 17.4 percent share of the market, but he said that Classic was gaining so rapidly that 1986 rankings would be very close. In other words, Classic might overtake Pepsi in the total market.

Beverage World, a leading trade journal, which computed its figures in a less complicated way, ranked Pepsi first, with a 17.6 percent share of the market. More significant, Classic is number two, at 17.3 percent, even though it was unavailable for two months of the year. *Beverage World* ranks new Coke fourth, with a 6 percent share. The trade journal reported that the combined volume of new Coke and Classic was 1 percent more than Coke's 1984 total.

Coca-Cola finally admitted that in the total market, Classic was outselling new Coke by about three to one, and by two to one in supermarkets. In the fountain market, they said, the two colas were about even; but in the spring of 1986, McDonald's, the largest dispenser of Coke, switched its 7,000 restaurants to Classic from new Coke, as did Hardee's, with its 2,600 outlets —a crippling blow to new Coke's projections of success.

Even before this happened, however, *Advertising Age,* in its January 27, 1986, issue, reported that in many major markets Classic was outselling new Coke by substantial margins: 8 to 1 in New York; 8 to 1 in Dallas, 9 to 1 in Minneapolis; but only 1.5 to 1 in Chicago and 2.5 to 1 in Denver. The trade journal reported that in Detroit new Coke was outselling Classic, but old Coke has never dominated that market in recent history.

As for public perception of the company, Coca-Cola proudly reports that its image was enhanced by the events of 1985. Prior to new Coke's introduction, the research firm Audits & Surveys showed Coke's image was less popular with consumers than Pepsi's. Using Pepsi's ranking as an index of 100, in April 1985, Coke's image was 89. In December of 1985, Coke's image was 120—a complete reversal.

More important was the company's stock price, which rose from $61.875 at the beginning of 1985 to close the year at $84.50, for an increase of 35.5 percent. By early 1986, Coca-Cola's stock had risen to an all-time high of $110. At that time the stock price took on special significance because the board of directors awarded Goizueta and Keough extraordinary bonuses. In addition to his salary, annual bonus, and long-term-incentive bonuses totaling $1.7 million, Goizueta was awarded 120,000 "performance units," equal to the increase in price of the company's stock over $61.875. While the value of Goizueta's performance units will not be calculated until the beginning of 1991, just based on the stock's price in early 1986, the bonus represents a potential of more than $5 million. Keough was awarded 65,000 performance units, potentially worth more than $3 million. Although Coca-Cola split its stock three-for-one in July 1986, thereby reducing the price to under this $61.875 benchmark, the performance units will be adjusted accordingly.

The company's 1986 proxy statement said these awards were given for Goizueta's and Keough's "singular courage, wisdom, and commitment in making certain decisions in 1985 which entailed considerable business risks, the net result of which has been, and will continue to be, extremely beneficial to the share-holders of the company."

These were the only extraordinary bonuses given as a result of the new-Coke-and-Classic strategy. Ike Herbert received a 5 percent increase in salary, but his long-term incentive award actually decreased 10 percent from its level of the previous year. Dyson's salary is not listed in the proxy.

*   *   *

As the two cola giants entered 1986, the game of one-upmanship continued. On January 24, following several weeks of speculation on Wall Street, Pepsi announced it would purchase the third-largest soft-drink firm, 7-Up, for $380 million. This move would increase its share of the overall market from 28 to 35 percent, a very close second to Coca-Cola's proudly held corporate leadership of 39 percent.

Not to be outdone or to allow Pepsi to breathe that closely down its neck, Coca-Cola announced three weeks later that it would purchase the fourth-largest soft-drink firm, Dr Pepper Company, for $470 million. That acquisition would boost Coca-Cola's corporate market share, based on 1985 figures, to around 46 percent.

Coca-Cola's latest move was based on several calculations, including data showing that Dr Pepper has been growing, while 7-Up has been losing share. Coca-Cola, therefore, would not have to turn around a faltering product. Furthermore, the Justice Department's antitrust division or the Federal Trade Commission could hardly approve Pepsi's purchase without also allowing Coca-Cola's. If Justice turned them both down, Coca-Cola would still hold a commanding lead in corporate market share, something it doesn't intend to lose, particularly since losing the brand leadership race to Pepsi.

In June, the FTC ruled it would oppose Coca-Cola's intended purchase of Dr Pepper, as well as Pepsi-Cola's proposed acquisition of the 7-Up Company. The Philip Morris Companies, 7-Up's parent company, then said it was no longer seeking an agreement with Pepsi but would look for another buyer. Coca-Cola and Dr Pepper said they would wage a legal battle to consummate their merger.

At the same time, Coca-Cola reversed a century-old policy of fostering an almost totally independent bottling system. It announced it would pay $1.4 billion for its largest bottling franchise, the JTL Corporation, the company owned by the family of John Lupton, grandson of one of the original bottlers. Its operations are primarily in Florida, Texas, Colorado, and Arizona.

Two weeks earlier Coca-Cola had announced the acquisition of the Coke bottling operations of the Beatrice Companies for $1 billion. Beatrice's bottling operations are primarily in Los Angeles, San Diego, Las Vegas, Iowa, and Vancouver Island in British Columbia.

Together with Coca-Cola's own bottling operations, these acquisitions would give Coca-Cola about 31 percent of its own bottling business. These bottling operations will be spun off into a separate public company but will still be controlled by the Coca-Cola Company. The new company will become very active in acquiring more and more bottling franchises.

Later in the summer of 1986—one year after the summer of its discontent—the company announced that Brian Dyson would leave his position at USA to head up this new bottling company.

Sergio Zyman resigned from the company in July to pursue investment opportunities.

As Coca-Cola entered its second hundred years, the company had learned that though risk-taking could pay off, as it had in several instances, it also entailed considerable danger. A gutsy management team could roll the dice once too often. Backed by the most expensive and sophisticated research in the com-

pany's history, the final result of the new Coke–old Coke episode was that millions of dollars and countless hours of staff
time were spent just to launch what may become just another
soft drink.

On the other hand, if you remember other product launch-
ings, like the Edsel or IBM's PC Junior, and think of what a
disaster Coca-Cola's historic launch could have been, then the
management of the company must be given high marks for
having the good sense to respond so quickly to what the
American people wanted—their own Coke, the real Coke, the
real thing.

NOTES

The primary source for the material in this book is the hundreds of hours of interviews with the major characters portrayed in it. The author also had the usual access to annual reports and proxy statements, as well as records and videotapes of such advertising campaigns as the initial Pepsi Challenge ads and Coca-Cola's early response. In addition, the author has drawn upon the information and understanding he acquired from reporting on the Coca-Cola Company since 1981.

Total market share numbers used throughout the text were compiled by John Maxwell, a leading beverage-industry authority whose annual report appears in *Beverage Industry* magazine. Supermarket share numbers were compiled by A. C. Nielsen Co. and supplied to the author by both Pepsi-Cola and Coca-Cola.

Additional background material and sources not specifically cited in the text are as follows:

CHAPTER 2

The recollections of Joseph W. Jones, Robert W. Woodruff's assistant from 1946 until 1985. Jones, at the time of his retirement from the Coca-Cola board of directors in 1986, was a senior vice president and assistant treasurer of the company.

"Boss Emeritus," a biographical brochure published by the Coca-Coca Company in 1984 at the time of Woodruff's retirement from the board of directors.

"Bob Woodruff at 91: The Old Salesman," by John Huey, a March 9, 1981, *Wall Street Journal* profile of "the boss."

"Robert Woodruff—Legend of American Business," by Raleigh Bryans, the March 8, 1985, obituary of Woodruff in *The Atlanta Journal* and *The Atlanta Constitution.*

"The Chronicle of Coca-Cola," a 1982 brochure published by the company.

CHAPTER 3

"Goizueta Brings Own Bold Flavor to Coke," by Sam Heys, a May 26, 1985, profile in *The Atlanta Journal* and *The Atlanta Constitution.*

CHAPTER 4

"Pepsi's Long March Toward Victory," by Richard Morgan, an August 19, 1985, *Adweek* magazine special report on the beverage industry.

CHAPTER 5

"Goizueta Brings Own Bold Flavor to Coke," by Sam Heys, May 26, 1985, *Atlanta Journal and Constitution.*

Goizueta's February 2, 1982, Management Stewardship Report for 1981 to the board of directors.

Goizueta's December 3, 1985, annual report to the "Coca-Cola Grads," a group of retired employees.

CHAPTER 6

"The Man Who Scored in Coca-Columbia," by Shawn Tully, in the February 22, 1982, *Fortune* magazine.

"Will Coke Go Better with Columbia?," by Jack Egan, in the February 1, 1982, edition of *New York* magazine.

"Herbert A. Allen's Firm Has Its Setbacks But Its Record Is the Envy of Wall Street," by Stephen Grover, in the July 22, 1982, edition of the *Wall Street Journal.*

Goizueta's February 20, 1986, Management Stewardship Report for 1985 to the board of directors.

CHAPTER 8

John Maxwell's market-share numbers.

"How McCann Kept the Coke Secret," by Nancy Giges, in the April 29, 1985, edition of *Advertising Age*.

CHAPTERS 10 AND 11

"The New Coke Introduction: Industry and Consumer Affairs Support," a report by Roger Nunley, manager of Coca-Cola USA's industry and consumer affairs department. The letters from consumers were supplied by Nunley's department.

"Pepsi's Sweet Revenge," by Bernice Kanner, in the July 29, 1985, edition of *New York* magazine.

ABOUT THE AUTHOR

THOMAS OLIVER is a native of Atlanta, Georgia, Coke's hometown, and a staff writer for *The Atlanta Journal* and *The Atlanta Constitution*. He has been writing on financial subjects for six years and has covered the Coca-Cola Company during that time.